Turning On Trump
One Tea Party Leader's Evolution

William T. Hennessy

The Hennessy Group LLC

Eureka, Missouri

Copyright © 2015-2016 William T. Hennessy

All rights reserved.

ISBN: 1533313598
ISBN-13: 978-1533313591

DEDICATION

To my wife who puts up with my moody inconsistencies and melodramatic narcissism.

This book is dedicated to the millions of men and women who served the cause of freedom and liberty in the Tea Party uprisings of 2009 and 2010. Your devotion to our country and our ideals will live on in history to the end of the republic. May we never live to see its end.

CONTENTS

Dedication iii
Acknowledgments i
Foreword 1

Trump, The Clown 10
We Deserve Better 10
What Good Issued From the Candidate Debate? . 13
What Is The Difference Between Leadership and Service? 17
Who's Really Left in the GOP Field? 20
Trump: Good, Bad, and Ugly 24
Republicans Worst-Case Scenario? 30
Trump: The final nail in the conservative coffin? . 33
I hate writing this post 36
The Debate for Bad Journalists 38
America is for Americans 42
The GOP Establishment Is a Cancer on America 47

Trump, The Party Crasher 53
It's Time to Choose 54
Party Like It's 1992 59
The Centre Cannot Hold 65
Bill Cosby Should Ask for a Change of Venue to Cologne Germany 73
White Water/Black Ops 77
Why *National Review*'s Trump Issue Will Fail 81
How late-deciders are like fish 85
NRO: Against Jefferson 89
The biggest shock in Iowa 95
This is the Gen X election 96

Trump, The Champion 103
Trump's South Carolina win was impressive 103
I bet Donald Trump reads my blog 105
A crushing defeat for Glenn Beck 111
How bad would Trump presidency be? 113
Trump knocks Rubio out of the news cycle 120
I'm trying to write the truth 123
The Psychology of The Inevitable 128
For Trump 134
An Affair to Dismember (Trump) 136
World Leaders and Paul Ryan Begin Negotiating With Trump 138
Trump for President. I Endorse. 140
Who Is Conservative? 144
Trump Is the Only Viable Pro-Life Choice 148
Here's How the Ryan-Trump Meeting Ends 150
How to Predict Trump's Landslide Win 153

Afterword 161

Works Cited 164

About The Author 171

ACKNOWLEDGMENTS

This is the fifth and largest book I have published. I think it's also the best. It's the best because of the great friends who pitched in and helped.

The cover design, which I love, is the work of lindagraphix. You, too, can benefit from her great work on fiverr.com.

Ben Murphy was Trump before Trump was Trump. He was the first person to review this book in its ugly, early stages, and he provided excellent guidance from the start.

Laura M. Wilkinson (lmwilkinson on Fiverr.com) agreed to edit the book. She is fast, reliable, and excellent. Without her, you'd have been confused by my missing words and vague references. Thank you, Laura.

Author and former CIA field officer John Braddock persuaded me to publish this book. And he is such a humanitarian that he provided key insights to make the book readable. If you like this book, as you probably will, thank John by checking his wonderful book The Spy's Guide to Thinking.

My nephew and friend Scott Evans, a master salesman, took the time to read my manuscript despite his exhaustingly busy life with three children. His suggestions helped me implement Mr. Braddock's recommendations.

Dottie Bailey, one of the fiercest champions of freedom, was also my first friend to jump on the Trump bandwagon very early. Unlike many of my friends, she never let my anti-Trump attitudes diminish our friendship. Her advice and skilled questioning, no doubt developed as the top salesperson in her field, played a critical role in the

thinking evolution described in this book.
Ed Martin, President of the Eagle Forum, was another early adopter of Trumpism. He, too, let me wander in the desert for months without criticizing or scolding. And he has provided great clarity in how to think about Trump.

Christina Bottieri is one of the greatest Tea Partiers ever. She is a wise advisor and a fierce advocate for our most important values. And she uses her remarkable powers of connecting and marketing to promote helpless waifs like me. She is probably the reason you're reading this book right now.

Many others helped, too. State Senator John Lamping has helped in so many ways. State Senator John Loudon and Dr. Gina Loudon are always helpful and encouraging. Michelle Moore, John Burns, and Ed Schultz are the political friends everyone needs.

Ben Evans, my consiglieri, keeps me sane and out of jail (mostly). And The Editor, Jim Durbin, has moved mountains for me and so many others. And Jim Hoft, the Gateway Pundit, is the best publicist anyone could ask for.

My kids, Jack, Ben, Samantha, Patrick, and Jordan had do without my wit and good advice while I pounded this out. They're great kids dedicated to making America great again.

Finally, my wife, Angela, will probably hate this book. I've spent hours in my office ignoring her to get this to market. She took care of things while I worked. Without her, neither the original blog posts nor this compilation would be possible. And without the future we want for ourselves and our five amazing kids, this effort would be unnecessary. I love you.

FOREWORD

I was one of the founders of the Tea Party movement. Some people think that fact makes my Trump conversion relevant. Or so I've been told. My view of Trump has turned 180 degrees in the nine months since he announced his candidacy in June 2015. People want to know why. People say, "Hennessy, have you lost your mind?"

Probably. Keep reading, you'll know soon enough.

As a constitutionalist, I should be repulsed by Trump's ad hoc approach to governance. And Trump did repulse me for much of the year 2015.

But world events and my own self-examination softened my opinion of Trump, and I ended up endorsing his candidacy after his chief rival, Senator Ted Cruz, suspended his campaign on May 7, 2016.

I compiled this book as a guide to other Americans who struggle with conflicting goals. On the one hand, we grew up conflating the Republican Party with conservatism and, therefore, believed the GOP was our best hope for constitutional fidelity. (That thinking might have been flawed.) On the other hand, that Republican Party has now nominated a man whose reverence for the document we hold so dear seems as sketchy as Trump's fidelity to marriage. Not only are Trump's positions on issues like eminent domain and socialized medicine troublesome, but the guy acts like a spoiled brat sometimes. He calls people names, he apparently mocked a disabled reporter, and he seems to believe provably false internet memes.

How could a thinking conservative possibly support a man who might embarrass the party, the country, and the conservative movement? If we had confidence that Trump's boorishness could lead to "a more perfect union" and a renewed devotion to the limited government promised in our Constitution, we might overlook his bad manners and those nutty pronouncements. But no one seriously believes Trump aims to impose Constitutional integrity on the federal government. Most people think Trump simply wants to enjoy the status of being the planet's most powerful man and the leader of the free world. In other words, Trump wants the presidency for all the reasons Jefferson wanted to avoid it.

Many of Trump's actions since announcing his campaign are inexcusable, and I will not insult you by trying to excuse them. In fact, I will barely mention them. Instead, I have selected a couple dozen of my own blog posts from the period in question, July 2015 through May 2016. These posts trace the evolution of my thinking on Trump better than any new writing could. They were written as events unfolded, often under the influence of powerful emotions and strong whiskey.

I got the idea to publish this book after an exchange on Twitter with a #NeverTrump person who accused me of "falling for" Trump's pretenses to conservatism. I never fell for such a pretense, and I'm not sure Mr. Trump *pretends* to be a conservative. Instead, he claims to be a fairly conservative person "in many ways." That's different, and the difference matters.

William F. Buckley's essay *Did You Ever See a Dream Walking?* tackled the differences between Conservatives, conservatives, and "men of the right" long ago and far more thoroughly than I could hope to improve (Buckley 1988). I'll say only that Trump is probably what he claims to be: a fairly conservative person who built a massively successful business, raised his children well, spends his money carefully, works very hard, and loves his country like a patriot. I will add that he demands excellent service for the guests and residents of his properties, and he does his own public relations (under an assumed name). In other words, Trump practices personal conservatism, the sort Benjamin Franklin wrote about in Poor Richard's Almanac (also under an assumed name).

I do not believe Trump is a Conservative. He is not like William F. Buckley or Willmoore Kendall or Ronald Reagan or even lowly Bill Hennessy. When asked to say something about himself, Trump would not lead off with, "I am a conservative."

And that's precisely why Mr. Trump won the Republican nomination for President, and it's why I believe he will win the White House in a landslide. That absence of ideological identity is also why I took the time to publish this book. Americans are sick of ideology. We want results. We demand results, and we are finally willing to roll the dice on someone as grating to our political sensibilities as Donald J. Trump. Trump's identity is not conservative; it's American.

This idea that Americans are fed up with ideology comes from Reagan's speechwriter and columnist Peggy Noonan. As she has so often, Ms. Noonan recently coalesced for me the idea that had been banging around in my head for at least three years. This rejection of ideology is the most important thing to understand when trying to Trump's triumph.

Ms. Noonan's column, the one to which I shouted, "That's what I've been trying to say!" is subtitled: "After 16 years, Americans have grown tired of both conservative and liberal abstractions."

Precisely!

That's really all she needed to say. The truth of that simple assertion is as profound as anything I've read in years. But one paragraph expands the thought.

Ms. Noonan writes about her talk with a roomful of activists. People wanted to know why, in Ms. Noonan's opinion, people are attracted to Mr. Trump. "He's saying he's on America's side," she told them.

> "And that comes as a great relief to them, because they believe that for 16 years Presidents Bush and Obama were largely about ideologies. They seemed not so much on America's side as on the side of abstract notions about justice and the needs of the world. Mr. Obama's ideological notions are leftist, and indeed he is a hero of the international left. He is about international climate-change agreements, and leftist views of gender, race and income equality. Mr. Bush's White House was driven by a different ideology—neoconservatism, democratizing, nation building, defeating evil in the world, privatizing Social Security.
>
> "But it was all ideology (Noonan, Simple Patriotism Trumps Ideology 2016)."

I sensed the same weariness with ideology in 2014. I sensed it first in myself. After five years of Tea Party protests, rallies, and subversive political action, I wanted to rest. To spur me on, my friends in the Tea Party would remind me of Washington's troops in the cold winter at Valley Forge. While the guilt-trip worked once in a while, it got old. Valley Forge was one winter; we were approaching our sixth.

But more important than my own weariness of action,

was weariness of the abstract ideas of conservatism. I still believe those ideas, but I am old enough—and I've been in this fight long enough—to see that shouting "conservatism" does not advance our cause. And shouting about our beliefs is about all we were doing these past seven years.

This book chronicles the lifting of the veil from my eyes in hope it might help you see. Yes, we want to advance conservative principles, but we must find a way to make those principles America's goals, not just ours. To do that, we need to stop leading with our principles and, in the words of Arthur C. Brooks of American Enterprise Institute, lead with the people our policies will help.

We haven't done that, and most of my brethren on the right refuse even to consider it. Well, Donald Trump's nomination is your wake-up call. People are tired of ideology, and they demand results. While we on the right were reading *The 5,000 Year Leap*, the American middle class died. Now, that murdered middle class rises from the dead like a ghost in a horror movie, demanding justice. Or at least action.

Trump is action.

I've organized the book chronologically beginning with Trump's first act, The Clown. Here, you'll read my angry mockery of the billionaire and his attempt to take over the party of Lincoln and Reagan and Kemp. The Clown ends just after the Islamic terrorist attacks in Paris and San Bernardino. If you're looking for a psychological hook, those attacks occurred about the time my youngest natural son headed off to Navy boot camp, joining his oldest brother Jack in the armed forces. The last post in The Clown is my reaction to Jeb Bush's attacks on Trump's modest proposal to suspend Muslim immigration until our leaders get a handle on what's going on.

Act two is The Party Crasher and covers the period in which I was examining Trump more closely. During this time, I re-read Trump's famous book *The Art of the Deal* and explored his most recent book *Crippled America*. During this period my view of Trump underwent a profound evolution. This second act begins and ends with, perhaps, the three most important stories in the book: *It's Time to Choose* and *Party Like It's 1992* open the section, and *This Is the Gen X Election*, closes it.

Trump's third act, The Champion, is the coming-to-life of Scott Adams's remarkable prediction from August 2015 that Trump would win a landslide. Adams writes that Trump orchestrated his campaign the same way movie scripts are written:

> "At the end of the second act, nearly all movies follow the model where some unsolvable problem rears its head. The audience must feel that

the protagonist can't escape this problem. We know the movie is fiction, but we still feel the emotions of the actors. We love the feeling of the third act because it reminds us of our own unsolvable problems. The main difference is that the movie hero finds a way to solve the unsolvable. That solution is what makes it a movie. The audience needs to feel the third act tension followed by an unexpected solution in order to get the chemical rush of movie enjoyment (Adams, Trump's Third Act 2015)."

Scott Adams says that Trump's third act began with his interview with long-time rival Megyn Kelly of Fox News on May 17, 2016 (Adams, Trump's Third Act 2015). But, for my purposes, the third act began when Trump dominated the Evangelical vote in South Carolina and Nevada. That's when I knew Trump's nomination was inevitable, and Cruz's strategy was fatally flawed.

My assessment of Cruz's strategy matters to some degree because his strategy was a general election strategy, not a primary strategy. South Carolina and Nevada convinced me that Cruz would have been destroyed in a general election. He simply misread the data. 2016 was not Cruz's year.

While Trump's third act will end with a landslide victory in November, I must finish this book before then. And you must prepare for what is about to happen.

Like Scott Adams, I am not smart enough to know whether Mr. Trump is the best person to lead our nation. I don't know the specific challenges and crises he might face. But I'm pretty sure he will win in November. And I'd like our side to hold some influence on his administration. Is that too much (or too little) to ask?

I hope this helps.

May 16, 2016
Eureka, Missouri

TRUMP, THE CLOWN

In the beginning, I thought Donald J. Trump was a clown. I laughed at him, I railed against him, I privately mocked his supporters. This phase of my Trump thinking lasted until just after the terror attacks in Paris and San Bernardino.

The stories in this section represent Trump's first act according to Dilbert creator Scott Adams.

Keep in mind, these are my blog posts from August 2015 in chronological order ending in May 2016.

In order for America to be made right again, she must embark on a 180 degree turn (to the right of course). Trump says he's the one that can do it. I didn't think he could last August, but nine months later, I made the turn on Trump. I believe that you will too.

We Deserve Better

August 8, 2015, 2:05 a.m.

What did you think of Donald Trump in August 2015? Do you remember what the polls said then?

I should have gone to bed.

I wanted to finish a great book called The Conservative Heart by Arthur C. Brooks of the American Enterprise

Institute (Brooks 2015). The book left me feeling happy, proud, and inspired.

I should have gone to bed as soon as I finished the book. But the feeling of having read something wonderful wanted to linger, so I sat with it for a bit. Then I really screwed up.

Facebook. Twitter. Donald Trump, of course.

Donald Trump told a reporter that Megyn Kelly had blood coming out of her eyes and "her wherever."

No, I'm not making this up.

Because of this, Erick Erickson rescinded Trump's invitation to speak at Red State Gathering on Saturday (Erickson, I Have Disinvited Donald Trump to the Red State Gathering 2015). Instead of acting like a gentleman, Trump attacked Erickson. Blamed it on political correctness and weakness.

No, Mr. Trump. Your problem is not political correctness. Your problem is that you are behaving like a buffoon. You may be a rich buffoon. You can take solace in that. History is littered with rich buffoons who left the world worse than they found it.

This is how Mr. Trump treats humanity. From his book *Trump: How to Get Rich*:

> "For many years I've said that if someone screws you, screw them back. When somebody hurts you, just go after them as viciously and as violently as you can (D. J. Trump 2004)."

So we know his nature.

A country reflects its national leaders, just as leaders carry the DNA of their country. Do we really want to live in a country where people "go after them as viciously and as violently as you can?" For slight offenses like asking questions in a debate? Or rescinding an invitation?

Look, I realize that a lot of good people got fired up about Trump. And it's painful to see the guy they picked to go up in flames. But it's time to stop defending him. It's time to stop making excuses for him. It's time to stop blaming the media for Donald Trump's infinite rudeness.

I posted this statement on Facebook:

"America deserves and should expect a president who epitomizes our highest standards. We all have flaws, of course, but our head of government and head of state should be a lady or gentleman, not a thin-skinned, jerk."

Mr. Trump had problems before the debate, but his performance in the debate made a mockery of the process. His behavior since the debate has been abominable.

I realize that some people still defend him, even to the point of blaming the 'hostile' press for Trump's boorish behavior. It's human nature to defend our positions, even when those positions are clearly beyond hope.

Mr. Trump is beyond hope as a presidential candidate. I hope my friends who have championed his cause will quickly sober up and quietly find a worthy object for their political affection. He is not worthy.

I also hope this post and my review of the debate will be my last mention of Donald Trump until he demonstrates the minimum level of civility and decorum America expects and demands from our national leaders.

What Good Issued From the Candidate Debate?

August 8, 2015, 5:50 a.m.
Comment: Did you see the first debate? How did you describe the debate? Who won?

Did you hear about the ratings?

Over 24 million people watched the first Republican debate Thursday. That's the largest audience ever for a cable program, save for sports.

Everybody knows why so many watched: people wanted to see a fight break out between Chris Christie and Rand Paul.

Donald Trump's presence probably didn't hurt. Let me clarify that. Trump's appearance helped the ratings. His performance might have ended his campaign. Donald Trump comported himself with all the dignity and gravitas of a George W. Bush as portrayed by Will Ferrell. At the risk of receiving angry tweets from Trump and his minions,

I tweeted:

> The best result of tonight's debate: Trump is done. #GOPDebate
> — Bill Hennessy (@whennessy) August 7, 2015

There's plenty of good analysis of the candidates' substance so I won't get into that. Instead, I tried to watch the debate like the majority of American voters. They don't like politics, but they figure it's their duty to vote with a bit of knowledge.

Who Else Lost Ground

Trump was not alone in turning off voters. Governor Jeb Bush struggled. He seemed a little needy at times, like a kid who wants to be left alone with his toys at his own birthday party. He defended his unpopular positions mostly by saying "I know better."

Senator Rand Paul, with whom I probably most agree, needs a bit more seasoning. I never looked at him and thought "Mr. President."

Senator Ted Cruz, I'm afraid, suffers with familiarity. I honestly can't put my finger on what it is about Senator Cruz that irritates me, but something does. Anecdotally, I'm not alone. When people ask themselves which candidate they'd like to hear speaking on the news every day for four years, Cruz won't be the answer.

Governor Scott Walker struck me as smug and a little arrogant. He memorized lines and recited them like a high school senior accepting his Prom King crown. And I so wanted him to do well.

Who Did Well

Mike Huckabee and Chris Christie performed well. Neither man wins on conservative values, but I like them more as people after their performance. Christie gets points for having the courage to propose changes to Social Security, which is an important safety net that's about to rupture from too much weight.

Senator Marco Rubio could smile more, but he seemed at times the readiest to be President. His speaking style would wear well over four or eight years of constant news about him. The panel on MSNBC declared him the winner by a mile. That might overstate the case, but he did very well.

Governor John Kasich might be the most electable candidate in a general election. He is smart and quick. His sarcasm comes across as sincere. He never seemed to be giving a prepared speech, which afflicted all but one of his debate partners. Katich will suffer in the primaries over

Medicaid Expansion, but he is very popular in Ohio, and Republicans will not win the White House without his state.

Who Won?

No one. But Dr. Ben Carson won a lot of hearts. He was the most human. Somehow, when he explained that he has separated conjoined twins and performed amazing neurological surgeries, it came off as an apology, not a brag. I believe his humility is sincere. His closing statement was absolutely brilliant, and the words themselves were too simple, the structure too casual, to have been scripted.

At some point before the Republican Convention, the electorate's mood will coalesce. After ten years of heated, cynical attacks and great suffering through wars, terrorism, mass shootings, and chronic underemployment that afflicts so many families, I believe the national mood will crave a human voice, a gentle spirit, and a confident smile. Those qualities will trump ideological purity and mad-as-hell bombast.

Ben Carson might not appeal to the dogma worshippers on the right, but he could win the love and respect of millions of people who simply want to get through life the best they can in an America renewed of spirit and prosperity. Sort of like 1980.

I'll leave you with Ben Carson's closing words:

"But I am very hopeful that I am not the only one who is willing to pick up the baton of freedom. Because freedom is not free and we must fight for it every day. Every one of us must fight for it because we are fighting for our children and the next generation."
–Dr. Ben Carson (Carson 2015)

Thank you for reading. May you have a blessed weekend, friends.

What Is The Difference Between Leadership and Service?

August 16, 2015, 8:20 p.m.

With this post, I tried to influence people's opinions of three candidates at once. Can you guess who they were?

Marine Corps officers eat last (Sinek, Leaders Eat Last 2014).

That simple insight inspired the title of Simon Sinek's latest book, *Leaders Eat Last*. If I could influence high school or college curricula, no one would graduate without successfully completing a semester course on that principle.

In a remarkable video, Simon Sinek discusses how circumstances can override our desire to lead and serve and how leadership and service can fix almost any problem

(Sinek, How Great Leaders Make You Feel Safe 2014). But first, I'd like you to think a bit more about these two critical needs: leadership and service.

America is woefully short of leaders. Sure, we have plenty of authorities. We have plenty of order-givers. We're chock-full of jerks who belligerently spit out directives of what others should do. But we're at an all-time low of people who actually lead.

At the same time, we have retained an innate appreciation for service. My unscientific survey of readers of this blog found that 82 percent believe a strong service ethic would make America stronger. That's encouraging.

What I think we fail to recognize is that leadership is. That's why Marine Corps officers eat last. Officers serve those who serve.

So many problems in America result from our leadership deficit. Do you think Barack Obama eats last? Do you think Hillary Clinton does? Or Donald Trump? I'm not telling you what to think, I'm asking you to really think about that one aspect of character and purpose.

Leadership is service. Service is leadership. Authority and leadership are orthogonal—one can be a leader without authority and authority without leadership. Most American business "leaders" lack any resemblance of leadership. They wield power. Most political "leaders" are mere authorities seeking only power. True leaders are rare.

But it wasn't always this way.

I had a boss who was a full generation older than me. We were talking recently about when business stopped being fun and profitable for everyone. His answer, "when the last of the World War II guys retired. That's when everything changed."

So many of those "WWII guys" knew leadership and service. They lived it. Sure, there were nasty bastards among that generation. But the World War II generation yielded a ridiculous number of true leaders. Bill Hewlett and Dave Packard, founders of HP, died in the simple homes they lived in when the company was founded. They never moved up. They ate lunch in a cafeteria with everyone else. Owning a great company never got in the way of their leadership.

America has a leadership deficit. To me, that's the most important issue in 2016. Without leadership, none of the other problems will be solved. None of them.

The good news: it's easy to spot a leader. A leader is the person who eats last.

Who's Really Left in the GOP Field?

August 18, 2015, 6:25 p.m.

Some predictions just don't pan out, right?

If you lack a unique, differentiating value, your only play is the price.

In business, you command the price play by being very, very big and very, very efficient. In presidential politics, you're unique, or you close up shop and go home. Commodities don't win executive offices. Usually.

Even though it's early, only four Republican candidates for president have differentiating value propositions:

Ben Carson
Donald Trump
Carly Fiorina
Ted Cruz

Everybody else is a commodity, especially Jeb Bush. (But watch Bush.)

Two stories put this idea in my head. First, Rand Paul's campaign is imploding. Second, Scott Walker seems to be imitating Donald Trump. When you're mimicking your opponent, you're in trouble.

I could probably make a case for Mike Huckabee being unique if Ben Carson were not in the race. Huckabee is a fabulous speaker, especially in-person. He has the best comedic timing I've seen in a politician, maybe ever. He's one of the few politicians I've seen who can deliver a canned joke perfectly. And he is sincere and humble in the process.

But Ben Carson is equally sincere and humble. While Carson may not have Huckabee's delivery (yet), it's impossible to disrespect Dr. Carson's decency and optimism. And that unifying optimism is Carson's differentiator. Dr. Carson is the most comfortable in his own skin of all the candidates in the GOP race. He might have done well financially as a neurosurgeon, but no one doubts he would have worked just as hard to save lives for minimum wage. His life's work involves improving people's lives, especially those with little hope. That's a life people can rally around. Ben Carson's unique value proposition is unifying optimism.

The opposite of humble decency is Donald Trump. Trump is just plain rude. He's the guy New York sends people to learn how to perpetuate the New Yorker stereotype. While I might say that Rand Paul appears unprepared for this level of campaigning, Trump says, "Rand's campaign is a total mess, and as a matter of fact, I didn't know he had anybody left in his campaign to make commercials which are not currently under indictment (D. J. Trump, 2016 Republican Presidential Debate 2016)!" Ba-ding! When I read that line, I hear Rodney Dangerfield's voice. Sadly, in the age of Real Housewives, egomaniacal rudeness is a differentiator.

Perhaps the most fascinating candidate so far has been Carly Fiorina. Her performance in the undercard bout last week prompted me to dig into her conservative credentials. I trust that she is authentically conservative. As I wrote yesterday, I have a big question she must answer for me, but if her performance to this point is any indication, she'll knock my question out of the park. That's because Fiorina's super power is communication. Carly Fiorina can distill complex issues to their essential qualities and explain them without demeaning her audience, even if they're experts. That's an indispensable skill for US President, if not for a candidate for president.

Finally, there's Ted Cruz. Cruz is probably the best-qualified candidate in the bunch. I should warn that "best-qualified" is not the same as "likeliest to win" or even necessarily my favorite. Cruz has a big burden to overcome—a lot of people think there's something creepy about him. That's his challenge to overcome. But Cruz is cool in an early 1960s Hollywood way. Like George

C. Scott in The Hustler. Not Paul Newman cool, but old school cool. It takes a cool cat to compliment Donald Trump when every political playbook since Caesar's says to pile on. Cruz's superpower is coolness.

That said, I still have a sinking feeling Jeb Bush will win the nomination. Yes, I said that Jeb Bush is undifferentiated. Yes, I said that commodity candidates don't win presidential primaries. But it's possible that my playbook is outdated. Maybe the power of money and monied interests is enough to overcome commodification in 2016. Jeb Bush is certainly the Walmart of GOP politics, and only a fool would bet against Bentonville, right?

I hope my playbook still works. Three of the four differentiated candidates seem like great choices for America. The fourth might have some good ideas, but a country that would have a rude egomaniac as president might be a country destined for a great fall. I wouldn't want everyone in America to behave like Donald Trump, but if he were president, we'd have a hard time telling people to eschew rudeness.

Go ahead and hate me, Trump fans. America must be bigger and better. Cruz, Carson, or Fiorina seem able to restore American prestige and prosperity without becoming a nation of jerks in the process.

Who wants to find out, after all, that the "shining city on

a hill" was actually just a louche casino.

Trump: Good, Bad, and Ugly

August 24, 2015, 4:25 p.m.

Note: See if you can detect a change in my tone toward Trump here.

There seems to be a certain air of inevitability that Trump will win the GOP nomination for President. According to a new poll, 57 percent of Republican voters expect that Trump will be the party's candidate next year. Why is that important?

Expectations Beat Preferences

Expectations are far better predictors of actual winners than preference polls. From New York Times:

> "Over the last 60 years, poll questions that asked people which candidate they expected to win have been a better guide to the outcome of the presidential race than questions asking people whom they planned to vote for, the study found (Leonhardt 2012)."

That study, by David Rothschild of Columbia University and Justin Wolfer's of the University of Michigan, is worth a read. The reason "who do you expect to win" beats "who do prefer to win" is because the former question effectively broadens the survey by a factor of 20 as respondents mentally poll up to 20 of their friends and family (Rothschild 2012).

Additionally, late deciders usually break for the candidate they expect to win by about 60/40, consistent with studies of other animals.

Brace Yourself

While I believe Trump's nomination could be bad news for the Republican Party, for conservatism, and for the United States, I do think Trump's candidacy has done some good. And I think Trump could evolve into an effective president.

So here's everything I see, good, bad, and ugly, about Trump:

The Good

From a sampling of Trump's oft-evolving positions:
- Political correctness is probably dead, and that's good thing
- The First Amendment is stronger because "offensive" speech is a matter of taste, not law
- There's a new determination to stop illegal immigration
- Trump has people talking about making America

great again, and that's what we all should want
- Trump has long decried foreign currency manipulation and unfair trade practices
- His position on the importance of work is excellent
- He says he opposes crony capitalism
- He supports a 0% corporate tax
- He opposes the mindless war on drugs
- He supports school choice and competition
- He supports domestic energy production
- He opposes environmental extremism while supporting environmental responsibility
- He stresses the importance of strong families
- He opposes Obama's Iran deal
- He opposes Chinese human rights policies
- He opposes warrantless government searches and monitoring of American citizens' communications
- He opposes ObamaCare
- He supports peace through overwhelming strength
- He recognizes the meaninglessness of official unemployment numbers
- He acknowledges that some people use Social Security Insurance to avoid work
- He supports tax reform and eliminating deductions, short of a flat tax

The Bad

From the same source:

- Trump supports high tariffs in a fragile world economy, which remind me of Hawley-Smoot Tariff Act of 1930
- Trump supports Affirmative Action
- He seems to support continued government funding of Planned Parenthood despite the organization's continued human right violations
- While speaking against crony capitalism, he has practiced crony capitalism most of his life, bragging that he "buys politicians" in the first debate
- Trump has corrupted the minds of otherwise sensible people with his birthright citizenship nonsense. Persons born in the US are US citizens with very few exceptions, like American Indians not taxed, persons under diplomatic immunity, and invading armies.
- Trump's immigration plan gives people a false hope that the immigration problem is easily fixed by executive order and legislation. It is not. As Judge Andrew Napolitano points in this video, every illegal we try to deport is entitled to a hearing and an appeal. The most such processes we've

adjudicated in a single year was 250,000. There are between 11 and 13 million people here illegally. As Judge Napolitano says, "do the math."

And The Ugly

From my observations:

- Trump encourages anti-social behavior
- He whines about "unfair" treatment from the press, and some people believe that's a sign of strength
- He shows little interest in fostering a sense of community and purpose beyond "making America great again" rhetoric. I am all for rejuvenating the American spirit, but I want all Americans to participate in that rejuvenation.
- He encourages a dangerous and fantastical notion that he can do anything as President, as if expecting some authoritarian or dictatorial power.
- He has inspired otherwise level-headed people to cheer on this idea of an autocratic President—even people who have for years complained of Obama's autocratic behavior. I would like the next president to prove Obama's autocratic tendencies an error of history. But if we replace an autocrat we don't like

with an autocrat we do like, then the precedent will probably be set for years to come. What follows our autocrat could be far worse than Obama.

My biggest concern about Trump is the Ugly. I think America needs a unifying leader at this point in history. On the other hand, I have a soft spot for anyone who earns the contempt of the Republican establishment. And Trump has earned that in droves.

From a policy perspective, Trump and I have rather minor differences. If I could influence Trump in only one area, I would like him to learn about conservative solutions for poverty and family breakdown.

If he winds up the nominee, I hope he will explain his changes of heart more clearly, particularly regarding abortion. His vague "I changed my mind" rhetoric makes me suspicious that he's simply saying what Republican primary voters want candidates to say.

While I appreciate his candor and lack of political correctness, he could supplement the strong language with clear and bold statements of positive purpose. He could, for example, stress that every person deserves the dignity of meaningful work. He could also emphasize that poverty and upward mobility are highly correlated with "strong, intact families, racial and economic integration, school quality, and social capital (like strong churches)(Chetty 2014))."

If Trump would augment his speech with positive ideas to rescue our most vulnerable citizens from the twin horrors of government and poverty, he could win over skeptics and critics like me. But to win me over, Trump will need to demonstrate leadership, not just chutzpah. We are at a time in history where we need a unifying leader who can inspire cooperation. We need a leader who eats last.

Republicans Worst-Case Scenario?

August 26, 2015, 7:27 p.m.

Another grand prediction goes down in flames.

Things are getting bad for Hillary.

I hear she's losing a lot of support from Democrat Party insiders, at least in private. The DNC is meeting this week, and talk will likely surround an alternative Democrats can vote for.

While Republicans enjoy the Clinton meltdown, we might want to be careful what we wish for.

One of the GOP's best hopes for the White House is voter enthusiasm. Republicans can't wait to vote, Democrats dread it. Voter enthusiasm influences turnout. A crippled Hillary probably won't fire up Democrats, boosting Republican chances in races from the White House to school boards.

But another candidate —or combination of candidates— might fire up the Democrats.

Suppose Joe Biden declares and immediately announces Senator Elizabeth Warren as his running mate. Biden would commit to serving only term. He would run to heal divisions with Congress. He knows how to get along with Republicans.

Meanwhile, the left would have their dream candidate as Veep and a shoe-in to take over the top of the ticket in 2020.

Biden-Warren would fix the Democrats' voter enthusiasm problem in an instant.

Meanwhile, if Donald Trump goes on to win the Republican nomination, the Biden-Warren ticket might cruise into the White House.

I could be wrong, but I think America will tire of Donald Trump's act. That fatigue could hit before Iowa or after November. But I bet it hits, and hard. High-intensity, overbearing people exhaust others, and Americans are weary already.

If Trump strings together early wins, it's possible the primary race will dwindle to Trump and Bush—the two with the money to hang on until the convention. With that choice for Republicans, Democrat enthusiasm would probably hit record highs. If we experience another financial meltdown, the press will demand Warren on the ticket. And the GOP will be down to Trump or Bush. (Never count Bush out.)

Charles Krauthammer worries about this Biden-Warren scenario, too, on Special Report with Brett Baier on Fox News.

Transcript:

> "He has an age issue which is if he were sworn in on inauguration day he'd be the oldest president by five years. With Warren, and if you announce you are going to be a one-termer, nobody is going to want to elect you. But if you have you as your heir, he gets the entire base, the Liberals have a vision of a 12-year rule, it would work perfectly for them (Krauthammer 2015)."

Look, I love seeing Clintons in political agony. And I can find good in the Trump message. But we need to be careful what we wish for. Biden-Warren would be a disaster for America.

Trump: The final nail in the conservative coffin?

September 10, 2015, 5:30 p.m.

Which stage of the Kubler-Ross Five Stages of Grief is at play here?

"So many battles are fought in war and in civilian life, and nothing is gained by their victory. Every battle we fight will result in a gain for us or we will not fight . . . There is no great gain in merely being right. To be right about some unimportant subject is not important."
–General George S. Patton

Jonah Goldberg explains the problem of Trump better than anyone:

"If you want a really good sense of the damage Donald Trump is doing to conservatism, consider the fact that for the last five years no issue has united the Right more than opposition to Obamacare. Opposition to socialized medicine in general has been a core tenet of American conservatism from Day One. Yet, when Republicans were told that Donald Trump favors single-payer health care, support for single-payer health care jumped from 16 percent to 44 percent (Goldberg 2015)."

There you go. If Trump favors socialism, then so do "conservatives." At least 44 percent of them. (Sadly, the 56 percent who maintain opposition to socialized medicine are more likely to support Jeb Bush. How far we've fallen.)

We hear, as Mr. Goldberg recounts that people who support Trump support him because "he fights." What he fights against is secondary to the fact that he fights. Apparently, conservatism now limits itself to fighting. Great.

But whom does Trump fight for?

We know against whom he fights: Fox News, immigration, and free trade. We know how he fights: insults. What we are not sure of is *why* he fights. At least I'm not sure.

And for me, everything starts with why.

Trump doesn't have time for "why." And that's dangerous.

Here's the danger: conservatives sometimes prefer fighting to winning. We sometimes choose impossible fights over winnable ones. We often pride ourselves in getting our butts kicked for arcane minutiae as if winning a lesser battle here and there is beneath us. (Wars are won and lost in the lesser battles prosecuted with vigor again and again.)

A few weeks ago, I pointed an instructive finger toward Arthur C. Brooks' similar concern:

> "[I]n a democratic system, the minority is by definition the opposition. Their de facto position is fighting against the ideas of the other side. Political minorities fight against something that's more

powerful than they are. And over time, their entire self-identity can become utterly reliant on acting like the principled underdog (Brooks 2015)."

In other words, conservatism could suffer from Self-defeating Personality Disorder, a real mental health disease defined in DSM-III.

Trump is the perfect enabler and exploiter of this condition. He proposes we fight battles an objective observer knows we're likely to lose, like citizenship by birth. He encourages conservatives to abandon winnable principles, like fighting Obamacare, and take up dangerous and unlikely causes, such as trade wars.

I'm not saying Trump *has a* self-defeating personality disorder. I'm saying he callously exploits the trait in others.

If the final defeat of conservatism is your highest objective for conservatism—if we must destroy the movement in order to save it—then your pyrrhic victory is at hand. A Mr. Golberg concludes:

> "I am tempted to believe that Donald Trump's biggest fans are not to be relied upon in the conservative cause. I have hope they will come to their senses. But it's possible they won't. And if the conservative movement and the Republican party allow themselves to be corrupted by this flim-flammery, then so be it. My job will be harder, my career will suffer, and I'll be ideologically homeless (though hardly alone). That's not so scary. Conservatism began in the wilderness and maybe,

like the Hebrews, it would return from it stronger and ready to rule. But I'm not leaving without a fight. If my side loses that fight, all I ask is you stop calling the Trumpian cargo cult "conservative" and maybe stop the movement long enough for me to get off (Goldberg 2015)."
God help us.

On the other hand, this is just my opinion. I could be wrong.

I hate writing this post

September 16, 2015, 10:48 p.m.

I was getting ready to head to Greenville, South Carolina, as a panelist at Heritage Action's Republican Presidential Forum.

I tell people I hate electoral politics.

Maybe I just want people to *think* I'm the kind of person who hates electoral politics. (We are all capable of being wrong about ourselves.)

I have to say, briefly, that this was the most encouraging Republican debate since . . . 1980? These are all serious people, and I'm including Trump. They all love America, and not just what they might get from America. Ya know, like the Clintons. These people love America the way I do.

I have no criticism worth writing about on style or substance of any of them. That's not to say I agree with isolationism or interventionism or the war on drugs or banning vaccines or minimum wage laws, etc. But nothing anyone said is worth attacking in writing. Even the stuff Bush said.

I do have ONE criticism for Tapper's questions. Every question was intended to start a fight between two or more people on stage, and most of them took the bait. Ben Carson, Chris Christie, John Kasich, and Mike Huckabee refused. All the others took the bait.

Ladies and gentlemen: stop taking the damn bait.

Now, the positives which trump the negatives by orders of magnitude.

I tweeted that I like all of these people more after tonight. In fact, after the first hour, I found myself rooting for all of them. All of them. I was rooting for Jeb Bush and for Donald Trump. I silently stood and clapped Carly Fiorina and John Kasich and, especially, Marco Rubio. Ted Cruz's presentation issues faded as he tired which tells me he needs to get less sleep; his positions are spotless. Ben Carson's humble decency makes me so proud and hopeful for America. Mike Huckabee—who has a lot of issues –is my favorite advocate for the issues we agree on. Scott Walker came across as a serious, intelligent man, tonight. Chris Christie's attacks on Obama and support of American strength were sincere and important.

I hope and pray that America watched this debate. I

hope and pray that young people watched. If they did, they saw 10 men and one remarkable woman who have put their entire lives in the public eye for the right to give us a better life–but only if we are willing to step up and live a better life.

My God, how refreshing!

I am prouder now than at any time since 9/11 or maybe the Reagan years.

Bravo, GOP. You have some wonderful people who want to lead and reform the greatest nation in the history of the world.

So, why do I hate writing this post? Because I sound like a GOP fanboy. But I am only being honest.

The Debate for Bad Journalists

October 28, 2015, 10:11 p.m.

Notice the long gap between Trump posts. Why do you think that is?

When Jim Cramer asks a question, you know everything's all boogered up.

The first hour of the GOP Presidential Debate from Colorado will go down as the first official event of the post-journalism world. The debate ended with John Harwood lying about the debate's length. Having been an occasional guest of Larry Kudlow, I'm being nice. But the CNBC reporters couldn't write a story for my high school newspaper.

On the substance of what the candidates said, this was the best debate so far. It was the best only because Ted Cruz, early on, scolded the "journalists" for their TMZ-smug, self-absorbed, unresearched, DNC-talking-point question. And Cruz informed the world that he and his fellow candidates would discuss the issues of the country regardless of what CNBC's nattering nabobs emitted from the festering noise holes beneath their booger boxes.

I'll be brief:

Carly Fiorina educated the country on what crony capitalism is and why it's bad for everyone. (I hope Ann Wagner took notes.) Carly did an excellent job of rejecting federal solutions to problems. While she was less in command than in previous debates, her answers were perfectly and uniformly conservative. And, as always, everyone knew exactly what Carly meant, every word, every syllable.

Ben Carson made himself even more likable, but he didn't make himself much more viable, and that's a shame. Dr. Carson needed to establish some degree of wonkishness. He has one more chance to show a command of his own plans or he'll disappear after Iowa. To be open, if the primary election were tomorrow, I would vote for Ben

Carson.

Marco Rubio was fantastic. While I have issues with his subsidies, he's the second-best debater of the bunch. And he probably ended one man's White House dream in the first couple minutes.

Jeb Bush is done; I think Jeb limped into the debate having recently laid off a bunch of his staff. He tried to regain momentum by calling on Marco Rubio to resign from the US Senate. Rubio unleashed a hornet's nest of facts and logic that left Bush nervously grinning and hoping for a commercial break. Jeb showed terrible instincts by taking on a great debater and brilliant counter-puncher. While Jeb's positions have become more conservative over time, his campaign is probably over.

Ted Cruz may have turned his campaign around tonight. His opening attack on the media was perfect. His answers to every question were excellent. He deflected attempts to make him look like a nut. If Ted Cruz wins the nomination, this debate was his turning point.

John Kasich seemed angry and distant. He was right about many things he said–the danger of scaring old people, the need to strengthen families, the realities of balancing a budget. But he delivered his message like the old guy down the street who doesn't want kids stepping on his lawn. I thought his performance was weak.

Rand Paul, I'm guessing, has decided to use the campaign as a platform. I don't think he takes seriously his own chances of actually winning. His reasonable and accurate explanation of the Fed's threat to the nation was perfect.

Donald Trump was very likable and very good. He got caught in one flat-out lie, but this was still Trump's best debate from my perspective. Ironically, I think Trump's bandwagoneers will see his performance as weak, so it could hurt him. Still, I'm beginning to see in Trump a man who could be President. Until recently, Trump's deportment was unfit for President. I hope the new Trump is the real Trump.

Chris Christie, I thought, had the best night of all the candidates. It has more to do with style than substance, but I'm betting the viewers will re-evaluate the New Jersey Governor, just as I'm re-evaluating Trump. His fantasy football rant was epic. Christie is the best debater of the bunch, and he's a genuinely warm guy. (That hug of Obama? Yeah, Christie hugs everybody. I've seen it.)

Mike Huckabee was delightful, but, like Rand Paul, Huckabee seems resigned to use the campaign as a platform for his views rather than a serious run for the White House.

As always, I'll steal Dennis Miller's line and remind you that these are my opinions, and I could be wrong.

America is for Americans

December 9, 2015, 7:45 p.m.

Another long gap between posts. Something big happened in between. Something personal and something much larger.

> DAVE: You hear from your folks, Mooch?
> MOOCHER: Yeah, my dad called. He wanted to know if the house was sold. He could use the money something fierce.
> DAVE: Well, you can come and live with me when it's sold. In Italy, everybody lives together.
> MOOCHER: [laughs] Since you won that Italian bike, man, you've been acting weird. You're really getting to think you're Italian, aren't you?
> CYRIL: I wouldn't mind thinking I was someone myself.
> —Breaking Away, 1979

> DAVE: Buon giorno, papa!
> DAD: I'm not "papa." I'm your god-damned father.
> —Breaking Away, 1979

Only two candidates actually seem to understand this country. (I'll tell you who they are later.)

To Jeb Bush, Lindsey Graham, and all the other candidates and pundits preaching the acceptable idea of America: you don't get to decide what America is; we do. Your opinion is just .0000000032 of what America is. Just like mine. America is what the people decide, not what Republican elites and the New York Times editorial board shove at us. So spare us your sanctimonious "that's not American" crap.

America is for Americans. What America stands for changes over time. But it changes because large numbers of Americans change their attitudes and behaviors, not because Jeb Bush releases a white paper on acceptable American beliefs.

But here's the bigger issue: America is not for Muslims or for the Irish or Mexicans, Norwegians, or anyone else. America is for Americans.

I realize that sounds obvious, but a lot of elitists seem not to get it. A lot of Hispanic activists don't get it. Fifty-one percent of Muslims in the United States don't get it. Hillary Clinton doesn't get it, and neither does Lindsey Graham.

Immigration serves one purpose: to make more Americans. The only reason to allow anyone into our country is to make it easier for them to become one of us by acting like us and broadly believing what we believe.

For the most part, immigrants to America emigrated from some hell-hole country. Elites in the old country boogered everything up so badly no one wants to live there except the elites. So ordinary Jordanians, Mexicans,

Norwegians, Irish, or whatever leave their native country for America—for freedom and opportunity and 24-hour sports and Wi-Fi everywhere and Black Friday sales on Thanksgiving Day. They come for 420-horsepower cars with drink holders and, yes, for the freedom to keep and bear arms and to write a blog post even if the blog irritates the attorney general.

The living generations of Americans—the people who actually decide what America is—we are thrilled to open up to people who want to live the American dream.

We want more of us.

We don't want people who want to turn America into the hell-hole they just crawled out of.

In the 1979 movie *Breaking Away* (Teisch 1979), the young protagonist, Dave, is a high school kid in Indiana. His dad works in a quarry. Dave is as middle-class, middle-American as a human being can be.

But Dave doesn't act middle-American. Dave acts Italian because he's obsessed with Italian bicycle racing. He wants to move to Italy to be more Italian. He doesn't want to move to Italy and turn Italy into Indiana. If Dave wanted to live in Indiana, there'd be no story.

Donald Trump gets that. I have issues with Trump, but he's one of the two candidates I mentioned above. The other one is Ted Cruz. The rest are too busy displaying their incredulity over Trump's words to remember that America is for Americans.

Erick Erickson is not admirer of Trump's, but Erickson recognizes this, too:

> "So, to put it another way, the day after the President failed to reassure a scared public following the second worst terrorist attack since 9/11 on domestic soil, Donald Trump not only got himself to the right of all the other candidates, but also got every single one of them for Sen. Ted Cruz to align themselves with Barack Obama (Erickson 2015)."

When Trump said maybe we should think about closing our borders to Muslims until we get a handle on this situation, he was saying what most Americans were thinking. What most Americans *hoped* someone would say. Not elite America, but real Americans. And we in real America have good reason to like what Trump says.

Most Muslims in the United States admit they want to replace the Constitution with sharia law. Most. Not some, not a few. Most. From a terrifying poll by The Polling Company for the Center for Security Policy, "51 percent of Muslims in America believe Muslims should have a choice of being governed according to shariah (Center for Security Policy 2015)."

In other words, 51 percent of Muslims in America want to turn America into the shit-hole they escaped from.

Suppose 51 percent of Catholic immigrants wanted to live under canon law instead of US law? Wouldn't we be very reluctant to let more Irish and Italians into the United States?

This isn't Islamophobia—it's defending the country we've built over 400 years. It's defending the ideals that go back to ancient Greece and Rome against a competing and incompatible set of beliefs.

When a majority of immigrants from an identifiable group says it wants to replace American laws with the laws that made their native countries unlivable, shouldn't we at least think about closing our doors to the people who identify with that group?

If you want to become American, do it. I actually think America needs immigration since the natives aren't pushing out many children these days. I'm all for people becoming American. I'm honored.

If, however, you want to mutilate vaginas, outlaw Halloween, and enslave or murder Christians and Jews who won't convert to your religion, stay the hell away from our country.

Our leaders have a duty to determine whether every immigrant is here to become an American or to convert America into something it's not. Likewise, the government must block entry to visitors who want to do us harm. We can debate the best means of screening out the bad guys, but let's admit that Donald Trump did us a favor by making people talk about solutions instead of admiring the problem.

America is for Americans, wherever they're from.

The GOP Establishment Is a Cancer on America

December 20, 2015, 11:40 a.m.

Before Never Trump, I was Never . . . somebody else. I was probably wrong about that, too.

> "Former Florida governor Jeb Bush, appearing Thursday on ABC's 'Good Morning America,' said that 'of course' he would back Trump, should he emerge triumphant at next year's GOP convention in Cleveland. 'We need to be unified, we need to win,' Bush said."
> –The Washington Post, September 3, 2015

The Republican Establishment has exposed itself as a political disease willing to kill its host. Unless we seek treatment and remove the tumor first. Some ideas below.

Here are three symptoms of disease:

1. Uncontrollable Bleeding from Jeb Bush

Jeb Bush is flirting with breaking his pledge to support the Republican nominee for president. And the only consequences he's worried about are the consequences to Jeb Bush. America can go to hell as far as Jeb's concerned.

Let that sink in. The man who demanded Trump sign a pledge to support the Republican nominee will break the very same pledge if Trump is the nominee. Unless breaking the pledge hurts Jeb.

Got that, Republicans? "If you nominate Trump, we'll destroy our own party." Ace of Spades points out the blatant hypocrisy:

> "Thus the double-standard so many complain about: The Establishment tells the grassroots not to make demands, and to remain loyal to the party no matter how little of its agenda is pressed for, while the Establishment and the pampered corporate wing feel pretty damn comfortable serving up ultimatums and splitting from the party if their agenda isn't eagerly serviced (Spades 2105)."

For weeks, Jeb Bush has shouted, "Donald Trump is not a serious candidate." Really, Jeb? If Trump is not serious with 30 percent support, what does that make you with 3 percent?

Readers know that I have issues with Trump, but The Donald is at least 10 times more serious a candidate than Jeb Bush.

Trump and Bush signed the same loyalty oath to the GOP. Now, Bush says he might break it.

Jeb Bush has lost his mind.

2. The Republican National Committee

In a similar way, the Republican National Committee held secret meetings a few weeks ago in which the committee reportedly worked up plans to steal the convention away from Trump should he win the most delegates.

Mitch McConnell was present at the meeting, but he said nothing. He'll let the committee members do his dirty work.

The Republican National Committee has been radicalized for the establishment.

3. A Budget Deal to Eat Out Your Substance

And last we come to the Paul Ryan budget–a bloated, politically correct travesty designed to win favor with King Obama and Princess Pelosi. The GOP Budget drove conservative icon Phyllis Schlafly to endorse Donald Trump. And I'm not far behind.

Conservatives complain that the Congressional Republicans refuse to stand up to Obama. They're wrong, of course. House and Senate Republicans will gladly fight the White House. They will risk a government shutdown. And they just proved it with this budget.

Establishment Republicans will shut down the government to protect their corporate overlords. They just won't risk any political capital for their hoi polloi constituents.

Corporatists wanted increased immigration and a lift on oil export ban. They got both.

Obama threatened to veto the oil export ban lift, but your friendly neighborhood Republican leaders stood up to the White House. If they hadn't, their sponsors might skip a $25,000 super PAC contribution or two, and no Establishment power-freak would risk that.

In the end, the Democrats got just about everything they wanted in the budget, as shown in this tweet:

> Rep Israel on omnibus: We ended up with most of the good stuff in and most of the bad stuff out. And that's a victory.
>
> — Chad Pergram (@ChadPergram) December 18, 2015

The GOP also funded Planned Parenthood, stripped funding for the border fence, and fully funded Obamacare.

And every Missouri Republican voted for the budget or the rule or both. Every single one of them.

What To Do About It

Unlike the GOP candidates for president, none of us signed a loyalty pledge. So let's begin by refusing to support or vote for any member of Congress who voted for the

Omnibus Budget.

That means actively supporting a third-party candidate in the general election next year if the incumbent wins the primary. Are you willing to do that?

It also means using leverage and making your leverage known.

In Navy boot camp, our company commanders (now called Recruit Division Commanders) used leverage well. They put the burden on the recruits themselves. If one recruit screwed up, the whole company (or division) was punished.

The system worked. Fellow recruits could punish screw-ups in ways RDCs could not. And recruits had more eyes and ears looking for potential screw-ups than the RDCs had. Thus, many screw-ups were prevented.

One way for grassroots conservatives to apply leverage is to make a formal pledge and stick to it. Last year, I pledged to cast zero Republican votes in any race if Jeb Bush is the nominee.

My lone act of defiance means nothing. But one thousand people in Ann Wagner's district would. Ten thousand such pledges would cost several Republicans elections.

Loyalty Is Killing Us

Any conservative loyal to the GOP is disloyal to conservatism because the GOP is disloyal to conservatism. The GOP is loyal only to its sponsors: Wall Street, huge multi-national corporations, and large individual donors. Their sponsors have loyalty only to their own wealth. They are not ideological, but they pay for a lot of phony research designed to stimulate ideological passions.

For instance, three corporations–General Electric, Philips, and Sylvania– stimulated the passions of environmentalists by sponsoring pseudo-science claiming compact fluorescent bulbs are better for the environment than incandescent bulbs. In fact, CFLs do up to 26 percent more damage to the environment (and to people) than incandescent bulbs (Bradley 2013), but CFLS were more profitable for GE. Environmentalists were stimulated by research to work against the planet to support GE's stockholders. Since GE does not pay federal taxes, profits are wonderful things.

So, I'll renew my pledge: if Jeb Bush is the GOP nominee, I will cast no Republican votes in November 2016. None. My little act of defiance may not do much, but I won't be feeding the Republican tumor.

TRUMP, THE PARTY CRASHER

At this point, I was not yet a Trump guy, but I was open to the idea of President Trump. I had no intention of supporting him. Ben Carson was still my candidate.

I began reading Trump's latest book, *Crippled America*, and re-read *The Art of the Deal*. I read all of Scott Adams's blog posts about Trump's remarkable persuasion skills. And I examined my own evolving view of America's greatest needs.

When it comes to America's needs, we are a badly wounded soldier. A sucking chest wound, shrapnel, broken bones. The field first aid guide from the military instructs us to stop the bleeding, start the breathing, treat for shock. The bleeding is our power being drained away by the Washington cartel. Applying "conservatism" at this point is like giving the soldier a blood infusion before we've stopped the hemorrhaging. It's spilling good blood after bad.

We need to first blow up the political, financial, and media elites. That stops the bleeding. Then we need to restore our place in the world and restart the jobs-based economy. That starts the breathing. After that, our beloved conservative principles become the perfect treatment for shock. But only if applied in the right order.

It's Time to Choose

December 20, 2015, 11:25 p.m.

A friend of mine told me she read this post aloud to her family on Christmas. What will it mean to you?

I am a mess.

I am a terrible father, a crappy husband (ask my ex-wives), and a difficult employee. I do a lot of things poorly. Most things, in fact. Especially the things I "have" to do. Authority irritates me.

While I'm terrible at following plans, I write a week's worth of blogs on Saturday and Sunday mornings. The pattern keeps me sane. Or semi-sane. I supplement those when events warrant. Which isn't very often.

And I'm irritated when it is.

I'm more irritated when I have to blog about being wrong, or admitting I pre-judged something. So I'm writing now with a lot of irritation coursing through my Irish veins, along with some whiskey. (Excuse the typos.)

An email received tonight threw me for a loop.

Phyllis Schlafly has been one of my heroes since . . . I can remember. I disagree with Mrs. Schlafly on exactly one issue, which will remain between us. Like William F. Buckley, Phyllis is a conservative touchstone to whom we can turn with confidence that she will point us in the right direction.

As someone who's doubted Donald Trump's conservative bonafides, I was shocked to read this:

> "Phyllis Schlafly, an icon of the conservative movement who has been active for half a century, is warning the nation: Donald Trump is the last hope for America (World Net Daily 2015)."

Donald Trump donated a lot of money to the Clintons. He said nice things about Barack Obama. He promoted socialized medicine. He built his real estate business with crony capitalism. And Phyllis Schlafly is endorsing *him*?

I can't question Mrs. Schlafly's judgment. So I have to ponder the message.

Trump is the "last hope for America."

Last hope. Last hope. Last hope.

The phrase ricochets around my brain like a ping pong ball shot into a Pringles can. "Last hope."

How screwed are we?

My first real political moment was 1974 when Nixon resigned. Nixon was a rotten president who used the power of his office to destroy political opponents, take America off the gold standard, back out of Bretton Woods, and impose wage and price controls. The anti-conservative.

Yet Richard Nixon campaigned for Barry Goldwater at

least as enthusiastically as Ronald Reagan did. As Patrick J. Buchanan recently wrote (and PJ was there):

> "Nixon pivoted swiftly to repair the damage, offered to introduce Goldwater to the convention, did so in a brilliant speech, then campaigned harder for Mr. Conservative than did Barry himself (Buchanan, Will Elites Blow Up the GOP? 2015)."

As a Gen X conservative, I like to throw Nixon under the bus. But Nixon and I had a remarkable correspondence in the late 1980s. The Dickster even sent me an autographed copy of In The Arena. He wasn't all bad.

The true story of Nixon comes to mind as I read Mrs. Schlafly's interview. I'm reminded of the other hero of Goldwater's campaign: Ronald Reagan.

Most Americans were shocked to learn Reagan was a Republican in 1964. The insiders knew it, but the general population did not. Reagan was a lifelong union man and a Roosevelt fan. And a Hollywood actor.

Even Republican insiders wondered whether Reagan's Goldwater speech was sincere or theatrics. (I heard from a woman who was at the 1976 convention in Kansas City that Reagan lost the delegate fight to Gerald Ford because people doubted his party allegiance. He'd been a Democrat for so long.)

After four years of Jimmy Carter's ineptitude, conservatives from three factions took a gamble. The foreign policy hawks, the fiscal conservatives, and the moral majority said, "Reagan is close enough." The three factions pointed their spears at the Democrats, united behind Reagan, won 49-state landslides, defeated the Soviet Union, ended the Cold War, reduced the influence of government, and proved that one man could handle the job of Leader of the Free World.

Tonight we face another seminal moment in history. For all intents and purposes, the Republican primary is down to two men: Donald Trump and Ted Cruz.

Ted Cruz is the Robert Taft of 2015. Cruz's ideology is pure. He makes Reagan look like a squish. Cruz is brilliant. He sold our philosophy to the Supreme Court nine times. (Ted Olsen envies Cruz.)

If I alone chose the next president, I would choose Ted Cruz.

But I don't choose alone. I choose along with 320 million other Americans. I hope they choose Cruz–in their homes, in their congressional districts, in their states.

The Republican primary system is messy and difficult to measure. In some states, a primary winner gets all the state's delegates. In other states, delegates are apportioned according to the relative distribution of votes. And in some states, like Missouri, delegates are awarded by US Congressional district results. If Ted Cruz wins the primary in Missouri's Second Congressional District, he gets all of that district's delegates.

The point is, Bill Hennessy doesn't choose the GOP nominee for president. So I have to deal with the reality of politics.

And the reality is that Donald Trump connects with more voters than anyone alive right now. He does. Arguing otherwise is just stupid.

I have a lot of problems with Trump, not the least of which is that my wife and at least one of my sons hate him. Even writing this post risks a week of sleeping on the couch. But I type on. I type on.

Phyllis Schlafly speaks for many millions of Americans when she says:

> "He [Trump] does look like he's the last hope [for America]," Schlafly said. "We don't hear anybody saying what he's saying. In fact, most of the people who ought to be lining up with him are attacking him. They're probably jealous of the amount of press coverage he gets. But the reason he gets so much press coverage is the grassroots are fed up with people who are running things, and they do want a change. They do want people to stand up for America. It really resonates when he says he wants to 'Make America Great Again (World Net Daily 2015).'"

I hate to think America is down to its last hope. I have two boys in the US Navy. I want them standing as guardians of freedom, not as warriors in a last battle for a dying republic. So this is personal.

I'm not quite ready to declare my allegiance to Donald Trump. I am totally prepared to declare my alienation from the Republican establishment. And if Trump is the only man who can destroy that tumor on American greatness, I will become a Trump man.

If Trump's good enough for Phyllis Schlafly, well, maybe Trump is good enough for me.

I think we should reflect on the Reagan of 1976.

In America, there's always a second chance.

Unless we're down to our last hope.

Choose wisely, voters. Choose wisely.

Party Like It's 1992

December 22, 2015, 2:25 p.m.

Was Ted Cruz's "missing white voter" strategy sound?

Five for five.

The first five people who told me they supported Trump in 2015 also supported Ross Perot in 1992.

I realize it's a tiny sample size. Still, it's pretty clear that Donald Trump is the reincarnation of H. Ross Perot. Conservatives–all conservatives and all center-right voters– need to come to terms with that fact. We must also deal with the realities of the 2016 election and choose a strategy.

The Search for the Missing White Voter

While working on my story on Millennial voters, I came across this 2012 (updated in 2013) analysis by Sean Trende of RealClearPolitics.

Remember that Trende wrote this in 2013, long before Donald Trump emerged as a serious candidate for the Republican nomination.

Describing the demographics and psychographics of the 6.6 million white voters who didn't show up to vote for Romney in 2012, Mr. Trende explains the high correlation between counties that voted for Ross Perot in 1992 and counties that saw a drop-off in white votes in 2012 (from 2008).

> "Perhaps most intriguingly, even after all of these controls are in place, the county's vote for Ross Perot in 1992 comes back statistically significant, and suggests that a higher vote for Perot in a county did, in fact, correlate with a drop-off in voter turnout in 2012.
>
> "What does that tell us about these voters? As I noted, they tended to be downscale, blue-collar whites. They weren't evangelicals; Ross Perot was pro-choice, in favor of gay rights, and in favor of some gun control. You probably didn't know that, though, and neither did most voters because that's not what his campaign was about.
>
> "His campaign was focused on his fiercely

populist stance on economics. He was a deficit hawk, favoring tax hikes on the wealthy to help balance the budget. He was staunchly opposed to illegal immigration as well as to free trade (and especially the North American Free Trade Agreement). He advocated more spending on education and even Medicare-for-all. Given the overall demographic and political orientation of these voters, one can see why they would stay home rather than vote for an urban liberal like President Obama or a severely pro-business venture capitalist like Mitt Romney (Trende, The Case of the Missing White Voter - Revisited 2013)."

When we look at Trump's positions over the past 20 years, they line up very well with Perot's in 1992.

The biggest difference between the two is that Perot ran as an independent while Trump has stated unequivocally that he will run as a Republican and accept the results of the process.

What Conservatives Need to Accept

I realize that many people see Trump as a savior even though he is not a conservative. Conservatives who support Trump (or who refuse to reject Trump outright) must make the case that the most pressing need of the country right now is bold, unapologetic, patriotic action. These conservatives must believe that our pet positions on taxes, the role of government, and social issues need to take a back seat to the problems of illegal immigration, terrorism, and America's place in the world. Conservatives can also argue that the Washington (and Jefferson City) establishment is so corrupt and so out of touch that the most pressing need in America is to blow up the political establishment.

I can accept that. I can't make the case that Trump is a Conservative. He is probably right of center, so you can make the case that is conservative. But he's not *a* Conservative like Barry Goldwater or William F. Buckley or Ted Cruz.

It would be helpful if conservatives who support Trump would accept that their man is not one of them ideologically and boldly assert why they support him anyway. And it would also help if Trump's opponents would make the case against him with a little less screechiness.

As Trende showed in 2013, the road to the White House is tricky for Republicans. The GOP candidate will have to attract those "downscale, blue-collar whites" in big numbers in places like Ohio and Pennsylvania. They'll need to activate all stripes of conservatives: fiscal, Constitutional, evangelical, foreign policy. They'll need to be acceptable to libertarians. And they'll need to get back to 10 percent of the black vote.

Americans Have Never Been This Polarized

The Reagan coalition offers no instructions for Republicans in 2016. Not only have demographics changed, but history has moved on. There is no Cold War to win. The triad of fiscal conservatives, foreign policy hawks, and evangelical Christians has been further fragmented by strict Constitutionalists, non-interventionist libertarians, and socially progressive libertarians. The Left and the Right are more doctrinaire and puritanical in their beliefs than ever before. No candidate is "good enough" for most plugged-in voters. Instead, candidates are either perfect or perfectly unacceptable. The more these voters learn about candidates, the less likely they are to vote at all for a Republican. (I know; I've helped fuel this absolutism.) The greatest economics writer alive, Ben Hunt, demonstrates the problem with this chart from the Pew Research Center:

> "Greater income and wealth inequality reverberates throughout society in every possible way, but most obviously in polarization of electorate preferences and party structure. Below is a visual representation of increased polarization in the US electorate, courtesy of the Pew Research Center. Other Western nations are worse, many much worse, and no nation is immune (Hunt 2015)."

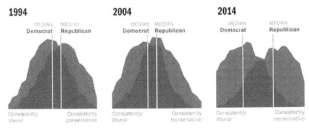

Notice how steep the lines were in 1994 and even in 2004 compared to 2014. The middle is gone, and right-of-center is now binomial (two humps). We were not so divided in 1980. As Dr. Hunt explains:

> "There's one inevitable consequence of significant political polarization: the center does not hold. Our expectation that The Central Tendency carries the day *will* fail, and this failure will occur at all levels of political organization, from your local school board to a congressional caucus to a national political party to the overall electorate. Political outcomes will always surprise in a polarized world, either surprisingly to the left or surprisingly to the right. And all too often, I might add, it's a surprising outcome pushed by the illiberal left or the illiberal right (Hunt 2015)."

Simply saying "Trump is not a conservative" doesn't solve the problem of getting to 270 electoral votes. Neither does saying "I'm for Trump."

To win the White House, conservatives might have no

choice but to work hard for someone who shares few of their ideological goals. Or perhaps Ted Cruz can find a way to inspire the downscale, blue-collar whites who eluded Romney and George H. W. Bush without alienating the other required constituencies.

Finally, another strategy conservatives can consider is to remain an ideologically pure, righteous remnant. That is a strategy, and a noble one. But don't confuse it with winning. And don't be surprised when policies move further from our ideal.

Whatever the case, the time for choosing is at hand. Choose wisely.

The Centre Cannot Hold

January 10, 2016, 8:10 p.m.

If you haven't read The Fourth Turning, you will want to after reading this.

THE SECOND COMING
 –William Butler Yeats

    Turning and turning in the widening gyre
The falcon cannot hear the falconer;
Things fall apart; the center cannot hold;
Mere anarchy is loosed upon the world,
The blood-dimmed tide is loosed, and everywhere

The ceremony of innocence is drowned;
The best lack all conviction, while the worst
Are full of passionate intensity.
    Surely some revelation is at hand;
Surely the Second Coming is at hand.
The Second Coming! Hardly are those words out
When a vast image out of Spiritus Mundi
Troubles my sight: a waste of desert sand;
A shape with lion body and the head of a man,
A gaze blank and pitiless as the sun,
Is moving its slow thighs, while all about it
Wind shadows of the indignant desert birds.
    The darkness drops again but now I know
That twenty centuries of stony sleep
Were vexed to nightmare by a rocking cradle,
And what rough beast, its hour come round at last,
Slouches towards Bethlehem to be born?

The Republican Establishment fears the party is spinning apart.

You probably know I believe in the cyclical history. So did Yeats.

Cycles of History

In *The Second Coming* Yeats sees the old order in Europe dying as the gyre (2000 years) that began with Christ comes to its end. The beast is Europe's ruling class moving slowly as scavenger birds wait for the beast to drop.

America has a ruling class—a cabal of political, business,

and media elite. On the surface, their factions war and clash, but when the lights and cameras and microphones power down, they plot together to keep the rabble in its place.

But that rabble is awakened.

The End of the Old Establishment

Maybe it was one-too-many hot mic accidents. Maybe it was the hubris of power and the ascension of elites less skilled in masking their contempt of the rank and file.

In the end, the reason won't matter much. The Establishment beast is old and weary. It's parasites look for new, healthier hosts.

The Democrat Establishment candidate has a socialist nipping at her cankles. The Republicans have no clear Establishment leading candidate, but a muddle of pretenders and wannabes sitting miles behind a populist and a conservative evangelist.

The center is gone. Not only is there a political center between the two major parties, but there's also no firm center within the parties. The New York Times article linked above explains it all in two short paragraphs:

> "Rank-and-file conservatives, after decades of deferring to party elites, are trying to stage what is effectively a people's coup by selecting a standard-bearer who is not the preferred candidate of wealthy donors and elected officials.

> "And many of those traditional power brokers, in turn, are deeply uncomfortable and even hostile to Mr. Trump and Mr. Cruz: Between them, the leading candidates do not have the backing of a single senator or governor (Healy and Martin 2016)."

Yet this isn't just about electoral politics. Look what's happening in the finance world.

Wall Street had its worst first week of a year in history. China's competence narrative is falling apart, and taking the narrative of the omnipotent Central Banker with it.

Wall Street and Central Bankers were key to the old Establishment order. The Establishment of both parties gave Wall Street a veto on their candidates long ago. Right now, the financial world is too distracted with its own problems to pay more than scant attention to the election. Besides, they have ways of making eventual winners see things their way, and they count on their financial threats to keep any new president in line.

The Trough of the Crisis

The Fourth Turning, published in 1997, predicted that America would enter a Crisis period within the decade.

> "A spark will ignite a new mood. Today, the same spark would flame briefly but then extinguish, its last flicker merely confirming and deepening the Unraveling-era mind-set. This time, though, it will

catalyze a Crisis. In retrospect, the spark might seem as ominous as a financial crash, as ordinary as a national election, or as trivial as a Tea Party. It could be a rapid succession of small events in which the ominous, the ordinary, and the trivial are commingled.

"Recall that a Crisis catalyst involves scenarios distinctly imaginable eight or ten years in advance. Based on recent Unraveling-era trends, the following circa-2005 scenarios might seem plausible:

- Beset by a fiscal crisis, a state lays claim to its residents' federal tax monies. Declaring this an act of secession, the president obtains a federal injunction. The governor refuses to back down. Federal marshals enforce the court order. Similar tax rebellions spring up in other states. Treasury bill auctions are suspended. Militia violence breaks out. Cyberterrorists destroy IRS databases. U.S. special forces are put on alert. Demands issue for a new Constitutional Convention.
- A global terrorist group blows up an aircraft and announces it possesses portable nuclear weapons. The United States and its allies launch a preemptive strike. The terrorists threaten to retaliate against an American city. Congress declares war and authorizes unlimited house-to-house searches. Opponents charge that the president concocted the emergency for political purposes. A nationwide strike is declared. Foreign capital flees the U.S.
- An impasse over the federal budget reaches a stalemate. The president and Congress both refuse to back down, triggering a near-total government shutdown. The president declares emergency powers. Congress rescinds his authority. Dollar and bond prices plummet. The

president threatens to stop Social Security checks. Congress refuses to raise the debt ceiling. Default looms. Wall Street panics.
- The Centers for Disease Control and Prevention announce the spread of a new communicable virus. The disease reaches densely populated areas, killing some. Congress enacts mandatory quarantine measures. The president orders the National Guard to throw prophylactic cordons around unsafe neighborhoods. Mayors resist. Urban gangs battle suburban militias. Calls mount for the president to declare martial law.
- Growing anarchy throughout the former Soviet republics prompts Russia to conduct training exercises around its borders. Lithuania erupts in civil war. Negotiations break down. U.S. diplomats are captured and publicly taunted. The president airlifts troops to rescue them and orders ships into the Black Sea. Iran declares its alliance with Russia. Gold and oil prices soar. Congress debates restoring the draft (Howe and Strauss 1997)."

Am I the only one who sees that, not one, but ALL of those possible scenarios has played out or nearly played out since the financial crisis struck in 2007?

That Crisis era, they predicted, will last about 15 to 20 years, after which a new social order will emerge in America. From *The Fourth Turning*:

"Before long, America's old civic order will seem ruined beyond repair. People will feel like a magnet has passed over society's disk drive, blanking out the social contract, wiping out old deals, clearing the books of vast unpayable promises to which people had once felt entitled. The economy could reach a trough that may look to be the start of a depression. With American weaknesses newly exposed, foreign dangers could erupt."

But before we get to the High, we will go through a climax according to *The Fourth Turning*:

"Eventually, all of America's lesser problems will combine into one giant problem. The very survival of the society will feel at stake, as leaders lead and people follow. Public issues will be newly simple [we're going to build a wall], fitting within the contours of crisp yes-no choices. [We have a country, or we don't.] People will leave niches to join interlocking teams, each team dependent on (and trusting of) work done by other teams. People will share similar hopes and sacrifices—and a new sense of social equality. The splinterings, complexities, and cynicisms of the Unraveling will be but distant memories. The first glimpses of a new golden age will appear beyond: if only this one big problem can be fixed (Howe and Strauss 1997)."

It's been nine years since the Crisis began with the fall of Bear-Stearn. Eight years if you believe the Crisis started with Lehman Brothers.

The Climax

Either way, we are inching closer to the climax. With Trump and Cruz running as much against the Republican Establishment as they are against the Democrats, the pieces are in place for the climax to emerge.

It's very likely that the 2016 election will bring about the long-term realignment of the social contract as Howe and Strauss predicted in *The Fourth Turning*:

> "Soon after the catalyst, a national election will produce a sweeping political realignment, as one faction or coalition capitalizes on a new public demand for decisive action. Republicans, Democrats, or perhaps a new party will decisively win the long partisan tug-of-war, ending the era of split government that had lasted through four decades of Awakening and Unraveling. The winners will now have the power to pursue the more potent, less incrementalist agenda about which they had long dreamed and against which their adversaries had darkly warned. This new regime will enthrone itself for the duration of the Crisis. Regardless of its ideology, that new leadership will assert public authority and demand private sacrifice. Where leaders had once been inclined to alleviate societal pressures, they will now aggravate them to command the nation's attention. The regeneracy will be solidly under way (Howe and Strauss 1997)."

When I read theories that attempt to explain Trump and

Cruz, I'm surprised no one else stumbled onto this one.

Like it or not, we're in the trough of the Crisis. And the worst is yet to come. Be ready to influence the new social contract. With or without a convention of states, America's social contract has been digitized and opened for editing by anyone.

Bill Cosby Should Ask for a Change of Venue to Cologne Germany

January 11, 2016, 2:31 p.m.

Sometimes I try to channel Tom Wolfe.

On New Year's Eve, male Muslim refugees rampaged across Europe.

They didn't use guns and bombs. They used their bodies. On women.

This created a political-correctness nightmare for Europe's leaders. On the one hand, the victims were women, and no means no, and we must always believe a woman who accuses a man of sexual predation (unless the man is Bill Clinton in which case we send Hillary to destroy the woman).

On the other hand, the assailants . . . no, no–assailants is too strong. The overzealous revelers were Muslim men and refugees. And Muslim refugees are safe, vetted, peaceful human beings who only want to adopt the customs and mores of their new countries.

In Cologne, Germany, hundreds of Muslim men assaulted hundreds of German women, and the German women refused to do the right thing (right by the political elite) and chalk the whole thing up to New Year's Eve frivolity. (What's a little grope between revelers, huh?)

Instead, these headstrong women (that's still okay to say, isn't it?) went to the authorities and to the press and told their stories of molestation. And they even went so far as to identify their attackers as "Middle Eastern or African."

But it gets worse!

The police *corroborated the women's stories.* Can you believe it? The police whose pensions depend on the favor of the Political Elite confirmed the victims–er–accusers' testimony.

What's a Political Elite to do?

First, **hold a press conference** and boldly state some platitudes. "No woman should ever feel unsafe, anywhere." "No means no." "Women own their bodies."

Buuuttttt...

Maybe women should understand that Muslim men come from cultures that value . . . well, other things. It's not really a matter of differences, so much, you see, as it is of *degree*. And these *fine* young men are our guests. And they've been through so much.

So I'll tell you, ladies, maybe you should think about how *you* might have, inadvertently, *enticed* these fine young men into getting a little too close to you and, well, you know, maybe these men–these fine young men–in all the bustle and jostle of a New Year's party might have accidentally bumped into you with all the drinking and chaos that goes on at these things. (Raves, I think the kids call them these days. It even sounds bumpy.)

So, here's what we'll do. From now on, you European women who are so well educated and so hip on sexual etiquette these days–so much more *aware* than our new guests from Syria–why don't you try to stay, um, let's call it "more than arm's length" from our guests, especially when our guests have been out partying.

Oh, and I know the new fashion is tight workout gear, what they call "yoga" pants and sports bras and all that, and I know you ladies want to look cool and trendy and all, but maybe . . . maybe when you're going out where you might be around our guests–such *fine* young men from very difficult upbringings–maybe you should dress a little less... *provocatively*, you know? More modest dress, like what these guests are used to? See, women where they come from, in their culture, the women dress *very* modestly. When these men see the way German women dress, well, is it any wonder they get over-stimulated? I mean, it's like the boys when I was in elementary school seeing their first National Geographic. Well, I'm older. You wouldn't understand that.

But, anyway, let's just call it all a big misunderstanding and try to help our guests assimilate by dressing a little more . . . you know . . . maybe wear a nice fashionable scarf on your head? Scarves were so elegant in the sixties. Think of Audrey Hepburn or Princess Grace. Especially Princess Grace because she did very well in a very different culture, and who *doesn't* want to look like Princess Grace?

Oh, and one last thing. Maybe, if something like this happens again, which I doubt it will, but if it does, maybe you could try to describe the young men–these fine young men–without assuming a country of origin or their religion? I mean, can you really *know* they were Middle Eastern or African? I mean, you didn't card them, I'm sure, and refugees don't have cards, anyway, but you know what I mean. Sure, they could have had a darker looking complexion than a typical German, but how do you know they weren't Greek or Spanish? So let's not jump to conclusions. I've been around some very 'handsy' Spanish men, myself, and I knew they were Spanish because they told me, but in a wild street party on New Year's Eve, well, I doubt anyone would just come out and say "I'm from the Middle East and I'm going to grope you." So don't assume.

It isn't very nice. It's not what a good host does, and we are, after all, their hosts.

And, finally, just to prove I'm not alone in saying we shouldn't just *immediately* believe the *worst* and assume guilt, I'd like to introduce that American icon of comedy and education, Dr. Bill Cosby.

Is it any wonder why Donald Trump's war on political correctness is winning?

White Water/Black Ops

January 12, 2016, Noon

Remember one of the last episodes of The Sopranos *when FBI agent Dwight Harris, who dogged Tony throughout the series, started rooting for the Sopranos in their war against Phil Leotardo?*

When I was a kid (even though I felt kind of old at the time) disaster movies were the thing.

Before Star Wars, the 1970s were about killer sharks, towering infernos, earthquakes, and capsized cruise ships.

Psychologists and sociologists attributed the genre's popularity to the people's need to assimilate nuclear holocaust.

I think the movies were just good, cathartic entertainment.

And then there was the more personal and mysterious horror flick.
WENDY TORRANCE: Hey. Wasn't it around here that the Donner Party got snowbound?
JACK TORRANCE: I think that was farther west in the Sierras.
WENDY TORRANCE: Oh.
DANNY TORRANCE: What was the Donner Party?
JACK TORRANCE: They were a party of settlers in covered-wagon times. They got snowbound one winter in the mountains. They had to resort to cannibalism in order to stay alive.
DANNY TORRANCE: You mean they ate each other up?
JACK TORRANCE: They had to, in order to survive.
WENDY TORRANCE: Jack...
DANNY TORRANCE: Don't worry, Mom. I know all about cannibalism. I saw it on TV.
JACK TORRANCE: See, it's okay. He saw it on the television. (King and Kubrick 1980)

When the Presidential campaign began, pundits saw the stars lining up for Hillary Clinton. (I didn't. But I've never been any good at seeing things in the stars.)

Hillary was running more or less unopposed for the Democrat nomination. She could pack in the cash and build an oppose file on the Republicans throughout 2015, receive her party's coronation at the convention, then come out guns blazing in September when people start to pay attention.

Meanwhile, the Republicans would rip each other to shreds. Seventeen candidates would make fools of themselves trying to tear down the heir-apparent, Jeb Bush. In vain, because Jeb Bush was invincible with his family name and endorsements and war chest. And no Bush has ever beaten a Clinton.

That was the prevailing narrative in May 2015. My, how times have changed.

Democrats will now run to RealClearPolitics and say "but, but, but the polls!" Yeah. Whatever.

The SS Hillary is a ship taking on water beyond the capacity of the drain pump to discharge overboard. The Andria Doria stayed 10 days afloat. I'm not sure the Hillary Clinton can survive 10 weeks.

Here's what's sinking the Hillary:

Benghazi won't go away

Hillary introduced Bill Clinton's unresolved sexual harassment charges, and the issue's not helping

Bernie Sanders only grows in popularity with the Democrats' socialist base

Political correctness–a product of the Clinton era–is a dirty word for most Americans

Joe Biden prefers himself or Sanders

Elizabeth Warren lurks in the wings

Jim Webb might run as a third-party moderate

150 FBI agents and DoJ investigators are preparing an indictment over Hillary's email server

Hillary's health problems won't go away

Fewer people are willing to say they won't vote for Trump under any circumstances.

Are many of these stories the product of wishful thinking? Sure. But not all.

And any one of these stories could stop Hillary dead in her tracks. If she loses Iowa or New Hampshire, or both, her campaign could be over.

Two years ago, I predicted Hillary would not run. When she announced, I modified that to say she would not make it to the DNC convention.

Look how the parties have reversed. The Republicans are down to two candidates: Trump and Cruz. And they're the only two who seem unwilling to attack each other (despite fraudulent attempts by the press to make people believe they are.)

And the Democrats are cannibalizing their own. Realizing that he has a chance at the nomination, Colonel Sanders is now battling Clinton in earnest, and Clinton is feebly fighting back.

The old days of the 1990s aren't helping. In fact, they're getting in the way. And her time at State seems more like time in in the state penitentiary. Her excuses seem weak.

Her plans seemed warmed-over. And she seems tired.

I stand by my prediction. And I'm more confident every day. Hillary will be nothing more than an honored guest at her party's convention.

Why *National Review*'s Trump Issue Will Fail

January 22, 2016, 5:30 p.m.

They. Don't. Care.

The conservative war against Trump won't work.

I get why *National Review* and *The Weekly Standard* devoted whole issues of magazines to Trump's lack of conservative bonafides. I appreciate it. Their work is important. But their tactic won't stop Trump. In fact, the fight is already over, and the cover story proves it.

Conservative magazines—online or on paper—are supposed to weigh events and people against conservative principles and pass judgment. *National Review* and *The Weekly Standard* are right: there is little evidence that Trump believes what we believe. And there is growing evidence that Ann Wagner's ilk will hook up with The Donald even before their divorce from Jeb! is final. (Poor Jeb! He was born with a silver low-energy bar in his mouth.)

I find it odd that very few people argue that Trump *is* a conservative, don't you? Even Trump doesn't bother much.

In his recent book, *Crippled America*, the word "conservative" appears only 15 times and most of these refer to other people or things. He calls himself a conservative only twice. Trump doesn't exactly kill himself trying to prove he's a conservative. He just mentions the stuff he does consistently that conservatives typically appreciate. Here's Trump's strongest argument:

> "By nature, I'm a conservative person. I believe in a strong work ethic, traditional values, being frugal in many ways and aggressive in military and foreign policy. I support a tight interpretation of the Constitution, which means judges should stick to precedent and not write social policy (D. J. Trump, Crippled America: How to Make America Great Again 2015)."

I won't point out all the ways Trump strays from conservative orthodoxy in that paragraph. That's not the issue.

If the political right is working overtime to convince you Trump's not a conservative, why isn't Trump (or his conservative supporters) working just as hard (or harder– Trump does everything harder than anybody else) to prove Trump *is* a conservative?

Because Trump's supporters don't care!

Trump's eminent domain abuse is appalling, and his support of the Kelo decision sucks. Trump's infatuation with single-payer healthcare sends Ronald Reagan spinning like a dental drill. Trump's trade policies smack of Smoot-Hawley on the surface. Trump's tax proposal has some unconservative features, and it isn't flat enough by a long shot.

And the people who support Trump don't care.

And they don't care that *National Review* knows Trump's not a conservative. It's like telling a smoker about the long-term health effects of tobacco. They know! They. Don't. Care. The "Trump Ain't No Conservative" argument shows conservatives are throwing in the towel. Dilbert creator Scott Adams, an expert in persuasion, explains the Persuasion Stack:

> Persuasion Stack
> - Identity (best)
> - Analogy (okay, not great)
> - Reason (useless)
> - Definition (capitulation)
>
> You'll see a lot of debate on whether Trump is a true *conservative* or not. That is *argument by definition*. It is the linguistic equivalent of throwing your gun at a monster because the magazine* is empty (Adams, Updating the Persuasion Stack (National Review's Trump Cover) 2016).

Unlike his conservative foes, Trump never tried to define anything–he operates exclusively in the world of persuasion.

As I've said many, many times, facts do not persuade. People reflexively look for errors in facts, so Trump wisely avoids them.

Put another way: Trump knows persuasion. Conservatives do not.

My conservative friends sincerely believe what they were taught in school, that you win an argument by marshaling the facts, that people decide based on a preponderance of the evidence just like Judge Wapner (or Judge Judy for people born after the Nixon administration).

But every salesman knows that's nonsense. We decide on emotion and defend our decisions with facts. Facts come last.

In the conservative war against Trump, conservatives led with facts and stuck with facts right up to the bitter end. Trump responded with emotion. And "make America great again."

National Review's Shock-and-Awe edition emptied their arsenal of facts. Trump deflected the attack with a single tweet:

> The dying @NRO *National Review* has totally given up the fight against Barrack Obama. They have been losing for years. I will beat Hillary!
>
> — Donald J. Trump (@realDonaldTrump) January 22, 2016

And with that tweet, the election comes to an end. It's 11:00 p.m. on Tuesday, November 8, and CNN just called it for Trump.

How late-deciders are like fish

January 25, 2016, 12:05 a.m.

Science isn't always right, but if it's all you have, you're smart to use it.

Expectations matter most in how undecided voters decide.

It's important to understand how late-deciders tend to vote. This knowledge (especially in Iowa and New Hampshire) could decide the outcome.

Primary voters tend to decide whom to for at the last minute.

In 2008, 16 percent of voters said they made their choice on election day. Which means we have a long way to go to know how Iowa will turn out.

I read a report that showed late-deciders tend to break for the candidate they expect to win. (Which may explain why most campaigns release a shock poll about their candidate's surge a day or two before the election.) There's also a study of how fish choose leaders which supports this theory via Science Daily:

> "Their consensus arises through a simple rule," said David Sumpter of Uppsala University. "Some

fish spot the best choice early on, although others may make a mistake and go the wrong way. The remaining fish assess how many have gone in particular directions. If the number going in one direction outweighs those going the other way, then the undecided fish follow in the direction of the majority (Cell Press 2008)."

But it's very difficult to know a particular voter's expectations, and those expectations vary widely by the voter's interest in politics.

Some late deciders are highly interested in the election while others are not. While less-interested people are more likely to stay home, many will vote. For interested voters, news and polls will provide a lot of information so polls will make a difference. For the less interested, personal connections and conversations mean everything. Even conversations overheard at a store can make a difference.

Who Will Win Iowa?

Looking at Iowa, it's impossible to pick a winner. It's very possible that more Iowans have made up their minds this year because of the incredible amount of press coverage, but the polls show that's not the case. The latest Fox News poll finds:

"A third of Republican caucus-goers say they may change their mind (33 percent). Even one in four Trump supporters says they may ultimately go with another candidate (25 percent).

"That's consistent with past elections. For instance, looking at CNN's exit poll from the 2012 Iowa Caucus (which Santorum won) we find Santorum won the Iowa caucus in 2012 by 34 votes over Romney, and his support surged on the day of the caucus."

How did Santorum do it?

Organization.

Santorum's supporters did a fantastic job of getting people to the caucus locations and of influencing fence-straddlers at the caucuses. My guess is that a bunch of that 35 percent who decided on the day of the caucus heard Santorum's name many times shortly after they arrived.

Does that mean the candidate with the best organization will win Iowa?

Maybe.

Remember, Ron Paul's campaign was famous for its grassroots organization, but that didn't help them in the caucuses. At the same time, Romney had a decent organization, too, but country clubbers might have shown less enthusiasm than Santorum's blue collar forces.

Cialdini's 6 Principles of Persuasion

So, besides organization and expectations, what else might influence a person to vote one way or the other this late in the game?

There are other factors to influence. According to researcher Robert Cialdini and his colleagues, there are six principles of persuasion: reciprocity, consistency, liking, authority, scarcity, and social proof (Cialdini 2008).

Clearly, social proof is the big deal in primary elections and accounts for late deciders breaking for the expected winner. But don't discount the others.

Liking is important. If a candidate's supporters turn off a voter, their numbers might not matter. Undecided or weakly decided voters will also pay attention to how candidates' supporters treat supporters of rival candidates. So treating everyone at the cause with respect might win some converts.

Likewise, authority can play a deciding role in elections. Low-interest voters might be influenced by one political celebrity's personal request than by 100 peers.

Consistency is very powerful but also tricky. For example, people who describe themselves as "very conservative" are very likely to support Cruz. But how people have voted before also influences them.

Reciprocity can help. Supporters of a particular candidate who offer caucus-goers rides or explanations of the process will influence people who feel they must repay the favor.

Scarcity is a little tricky here, but it's huge in getting voters to the polls or caucus. "This is your only chance to choose the next president."

We Just Don't Know

Which is all a long way to get to this: we won't know the winner until the votes are counted, and news reports of a candidate's surge can be counteracted by what voters see on the ground on caucus day.

NRO: Against Jefferson

January 26, 2016, 11:25 p.m.

National Review, the magazine William F. Buckley Jr. founded, decided to declare war on millions of American voters. Was NR right?

> "Aristocrats fear the people, and wish to transfer all power to the higher classes of society."
> –Thomas Jefferson to William Short, 1825.

National Review has entered dangerous territory: they have inadvertently made the case for Trump.

An angry screed by Kevin Williamson titled "Our Post-Literate Politics" (later renamed to "What's a Book?") makes the case that Trump supporters are illiterate, uneducated, dim-witted, racist, homophobes. To wit:

> "Thomas Aquinas cautioned against 'homo unius libri,' a warning that would not get very far with the typical Trump voter stuck sniggering over 'homo.' (They'd snigger over 'snigger,' too, for similar reasons.)"

And

> "Donald Trump is the face of that insalubrious relationship, a lifelong crony capitalist who brags about buying political favors. But his enthusiasts, devoid as they are of a literate politics capable of thinking about all three sides of a triangle at the same time (Williamson 2016)[.]"

The magazine's aristocratic editors have examined the species *homo trumpicus* and found it unfit for self-governance. Until last fall, *homo trumpicus* was NR's favorite fellow-traveller.

For those who don't regularly read Hennessy's View (and I seem to have a lot of new readers of late), I am not supporting Donald Trump. Also, I agree with the NR writers that Trump does not fit my definition of conservatism (which, like most conservatives, I cannot articulate in a way that you could a draw a picture from). Further, I'll give you that Trump scares me a little. Finally, on this point, there are at least three candidates I'd greatly prefer to Trump and a couple more I'd probably hold my nose and vote for before I'd touch the screen next to The Donald. (Or maybe he'll be on the ballot as simply

"TRUMP.") (And Jeb! is not one of them. I'll take Trump over Jeb!)

While I revere William F. Buckley, my own vision of a conservative utopia has been out of phase with NR's for some time, at least in a few ways. In 1993, for example, I wrote an essay opposing US intervention in the Balkans. I am proud that my essay was published alongside similar sentiments from Patrick J. Buchanan and Phyllis Schlafly. (Maybe it's a St. Louis thing. Buchanan cut his newspaper teeth at the St. Louis Globe-Democrat, and Schlafly is, of course, a St. Louisan.) I differed from my favorite magazine on the issue.

In 1994, a friend and I earned beer money by selling shirts and bumper stickers. Our best-seller said "He's Rested, He's Ready, He's RIGHT! Buchanan '96." (My personal favorite didn't sell worth a damn: "Why did I get wet when Clinton soaked the rich?")

I should point out that I have differences with Buchanan (Israel) and Schlafly (convention of states), too. But my vision of conservative utopia is probably a lot closer to theirs than to the current editors of *National Review*. And while I've dutifully bucked up and supported whatever lame Establishment punching bag the GOP sends up every four years, like many others, I'm getting pretty sick of supporting a party that prefers abstract principles and handouts-tobillionaires over sound policies that lift people out of poverty and give those well above poverty the confidence to jump employers, change careers, or hang out a shingle.

My view is pretty simple and probably more libertarian than conservative. I believe that free men and women, decently educated, reasonably honest, occasionally sober, and mildly ambitious make for an exceptional nation. I believe that a government that provides the safety and security to let the men and women have their fun (without feeling the need to wear rearview sunglasses in case some crazed Jihadi is sneaking up on them) is a government that engenders exceptionalism. (Unlike my definition of conservatism, I can point you to a picture of exceptionalism. It's something like Burning Man surrounded on each end by a week or two of hard work.) And I believe that an agreed-upon and complete list of things the government is allowed to do lets the people plan more than 3 minutes ahead, which is a prerequisite of exceptionalism, freedom, and fun.

And all of my beliefs are built on the idea that people, by their nature, can govern themselves. One requirement of self-governance is choosing representatives, including the chief executive of the country.

If I'm wrong on that–if people truly cannot government themselves and cannot form governments that function–then the whole concept of liberty and everything written on the subject from John Locke to Thomas Jefferson to William F. Buckley, was a lie, an error, a sham, a horrible mistake. On that point, Locke, Jefferson, and Buckley agree with me.

So yesterday *National Review*, in its screechy cat-fight of a hissy fit, determined that 41 percent of Republican voters (and 100 percent of Democrat voters) fail the self-governance test and need an aristocracy to rule them. Assuming half the voters are Democrats, that means *National Review* has written off, not 47 percent, but 91 percent of the American population. Nearly everybody *but* the *National Review's* editorial board is, by their reckoning, too ignorant and illiterate to own their own lives.

And this is where the fun begins.

National Review's anti-Trump symposium warns that Trump is a modern day Hitler ready to seize autocratic power in America, *and* that Americans need an autocrat to rule them in their vast ignorance and bigotry.

Put syllogistically (a word that should satisfy Mr. Williamson and most of the *National Review* symposium authors):

> "If Donald Trump is an authoritarian with conservative-ish pretenses, and if the American electorate's ignorance requires authoritarian rule, then Trump is the best authoritarian for the job."

I utterly disavow *National Review's* pessimistic, aristocratic, and undemocratic conclusion. I reject the middle leg of their pro-Trump syllogism because I believe we are competent to run our lives and to decide on a working government.

And on that, Jefferson concurs:

> "The people, being the only safe depository of power, should exercise in person every function which their qualifications enable them to exercise consistently with the order and security of society. We now find them equal to the election of those who shall be invested with their executive and legislative powers, and to act themselves in the judiciary as judges in questions of fact. The range of their powers ought to be enlarged." –Thomas Jefferson to Walter Jones, 1814.

Either we can govern ourselves, or we can't. I think we can; *National Review* thinks we can't.

But I admit to taking great satisfaction in the pain and suffering Trump visits upon snobbish blowhards like the one who told his readers that 41 percent of Republicans can't govern themselves.

As always, I'll end with the words Dennis Miller gave us: that's just my opinion; I could be wrong.

The biggest shock in Iowa

February 1, 2016, 10:08 p.m.

Now things start to get interesting.

The polls were wrong. But that wasn't the biggest shock.

The big shock was... who was that guy pretending to be Donald Trump?

Millions and millions of people waited to watch The Donald meltdown after finishing second behind Ted Cruz.

But it didn't happen. Instead, Trump managed to show humility and graciousness without giving up his signature bravado. Pretty brilliant. As Romney and Rove learned in 2012, though, air power will not win many races. You need boots on the ground. Cruz had them; Trump didn't.

A bigger shock: Marco Rubio's performance. And that's bad news for both Cruz and Trump. Rubio stands to pick up the lion's share of support from Kasich, Jeb, Christie, and Fiorina as they drop. Add 60 percent of those supporters to Rubio's numbers, and he's the frontrunner. Plus, Rubio stands to win a lot of delegates in the deep blue states (California, New York, etc.).

Expect the establishment and the media to turn their fire toward Cruz.

But the biggest shock: Bernie Sanders might have driven

a wooden stake into the heart of Countess Clinton and the Arkansas Vampire Gang. As I write, with 91 percent in, Hillary leads by 0.02.

Even if Hillary prevails, the margin of error will likely be less than 1%. She will do better on the delegate count, but with an indictment looming for mishandling top secret documents while Secretary of State (and repeatedly lying about it), Clinton is in serious trouble.

This is the Gen X election

February 20, 2016, 3:20 p.m.

A friend of mine tells me this is the best of my 3,000 blog posts. See if you can figure out why.

Who would have thought that Pat Buchanan would become the spokesman for Generation X?

I put a lot of stock into generational history. I am a big fan of Howe and Strauss, a pair of historians whose works include *Generations: The History of America's Future*, *13ers: Abort, Retry, Ignore, Fail?*, *Millennials Rising*, and, my favorite, *The Fourth Turning*.

As someone born in the 13th generation of Americans, more commonly called Generation X after the book by Douglas Coupland, I am overly captivated by that generation. My generation. The generation that was too young for Woodstock and too old by the time we turned twelve.

As a generation, Xers are iconoclastic, sarcastic, and just a bit nihilistic. (Our Boomer brothers and sisters grew up with bomb shelters to survive a nuclear war. We just looked up and waited to see the birds fly in.)

We rebelled against the Boomers' excesses, but we still bummed pot off our older Boomer siblings. We were something of an Eddie Haskel generation–clean-cut, polite, and well-dressed around the grown-ups, but we carried a flask in one pocket and a half bag in the other. We laughed at the Boomers who created so much tension by openly rebelling against the conformity of the post-war era. We rejected conformity, too, but we did it with more stealth. We didn't get caught. And when we did get caught, we charmed our way out of the most serious consequences.

That's just my opinion. Your mileage may vary. But here's how those masters of generational history describe the Xers.

> "The 13th Generation (Nomad, born 1961-1981) survived a hurried childhood of divorce, latchkeys, open classrooms, devil-child movies, and a shift from G to R ratings. They came of age curtailing the earlier rise in youth crime and fall in test scores—yet heard themselves denounced as so wild and stupid as to put The Nation at Risk.

As young adults, maneuvering through a
sexual battlescape of AIDS and blighted courtship
rituals, they date and marry cautiously. In jobs, they
embrace risk and prefer free agency over loyal
corporatism. From grunge to hip-hop,
their splintery culture reveals a hardened
edge. Politically, they lean toward
pragmatism and nonaffiliation and would rather
volunteer than vote. Widely criticized as Xers
or slackers, they inhabit a Reality Bites economy of
declining young-adult living standards. (American:
Tom Cruise, Jodie Foster, Michael Dell, Deion
Sanders, Winona Ryder, Quentin Tarantino;
Foreign: Princess Di, Alanis Morissette) (Howe and
Strauss 1997)"

That was written in 1997, by the way. I was thirty-three, Bill Clinton was president, and few people had heard of Osama bin Laden or Monica Lewinsky.

I realize Donald Trump's support is strongest among Boomers and older (60+), and Sanders's support comes from Millennials. But the reason these iconoclastic candidates are around at all is because the Gen X culture finally made it to politics in 2016.

Even though we dressed like Alex P. Keaton, our heroes were working-class American rebels. Our music pissed off the Glenn Miller and the Pat Boone generations, of course. But grunge and hip-hop also pissed off the Boomers. We liked everything hard: Joan Jett, Bruce Springsteen, Bon Jovi, Nirvana. The song I heard most in 1985 was a Dire

Straits song about installing microwave ovens and custom kitchen deliveries while dreaming about being a star on MTV. Everybody was working for the weekend, and the girls just wanted to have fun, and I had one hand in my pocket and the other one's smoking a cigarette.

Well, the Eddie Haskel generation, the generation that nobody watched, is now running stuff. The slackers are in charge. The principal's name is McFly. We hung around with the establishment kids in college (because they had cool boats and good drugs), but we never were *of* them. We ran in circles with the elites, but, by mutual agreement, we never got too close. And we didn't touch the fine porcelain statues in the foyer. (But we did hook up with their sisters.)

And now that reckless, dangerous generation is in charge–of business, of political campaigns, and of the media. Yeah, there's a lot of Boomers hanging around in the C-Suite, but the Xers are, for a short time, calling the shots.

And the shots we're calling are angry and risky, like a Van Halen song.

Torya Neumyer writes about the end of the political establishment that's held sway since V-J Day:

> "This cycle, dynasty hasn't counted for much. In the debate two days earlier, Trump viciously attacked the elder Bush's record, marking the first time anyone can remember a GOP poll leader

lacerating the party's most recent President. Trump earned boos for the performance, but the audience in attendance—South Carolina party faithfuls—was so distant from the Republican rank and file that the question "Why are people booing?" trended on Google during the debate. What's more, the businessman's soaring popularity statewide didn't suffer. If Palmetto State Republicans didn't punish that heresy against the last Republican commander in chief, it could spell the last gasp for Jeb, who finished 6th in Iowa and 4th in Iowa (Newmyer 2016)."

Punish heresy? Hell, no. Not in the Gen X election year of 2016. Heresy's what we gave up Lent for.

I'm not saying all Gen Xers will vote for Trump. I am saying the Gen X attitude that formed in the 1980s and 1990s has finally pervaded the generations on all sides. Just as the Boomer attitude hatched in the 1960s and 1970s, finally seized full power in the Clinton administration.

(George H.W. Bush belonged to the World War II Hero generation, as did every president before him, back to Kennedy.)

Nor am I saying the next president will be an Xer. That doesn't matter. Reagan embodied the spiritual awakening and suspicion of government that the Boomers launched, and it's very possible for someone of an earlier generation to animate the zeitgeist of Generation X. Boomer Trump is very much an Xer in attitude. So are Sanders, Cruz, and Rubio. Bush and Clinton typify the Boomer attitude which turns off Xers.

Maybe successful candidates need a bridge between Boomers and Millennials, the two largest generations in American history. And that bridge is Gen X. While Xers are too small in number to dominate an election, we're the conduit needed to win one.

Pat Buchanan sees the problem for a political establishment that refused to listen to us since 1996:

> "But while difficult to see how Sanders captures the nomination and wins in November, the rebellion in the GOP is larger, stronger and deeper. In every national or state poll, anti-establishment candidates command a majority of Republican voters. Which presents a problem for the establishment.
> "The Beltway elites may succeed in blocking Trump or Ted Cruz. But the eventual nominee and the party will have to respect and to some degree accommodate the agendas of the rebellion on immigration, border security, trade, and anti-intervention, or face a fatal split (Buchanan, Is the New Era Upon Us? 2016)."

After Ed Martin had decided to run for Missouri Attorney General to give Ann Wagner clear sailing to the US House of Representatives, I sat down with Ann for a few hours. Ann and I graduated from high school the same year, so we had a lot of shared memories of the time.

I asked her how she got into politics. "1996," she said. "After Missouri voted for Buchanan in the caucuses, I had to do whatever it took to make sure nothing like that ever happens again (Wagner 2012)."

I told her that I had a small business that sold bumper stickers and shirts. Our most popular item in 1993 and 1994 read "He's Rested, He's Ready, He's Right! Buchanan '96."

Ann laughed when I told her. Maybe she thought I was kidding.

The Buchanan Brigades are running the show, now. While the establishment could still produce the next president, he or she will be unable to govern, I'm afraid. The divisions are too many, the chasms too wide, the trust too broken, the economy too leveraged.

We've been warning the establishment for decades that we're not gonna take it. They didn't listen.

But something tells me they're listening now. They might even be listening to Pat.

TRUMP, THE CHAMPION

Trump's South Carolina win was impressive

February 21, 2016, 2:21 a.m.

Did you pay attention to South Carolina's primary?

I got tired of scrolling.

Politico shows the results of each county in South Carolina (Politico 2016), my state of residence from 1985 to 1992.

It goes on and on and on. You get the idea.

Donald Trump not only won the geography, but he also won the demography:

Evangelical Christians: Trump

Born-again Christians: Trump

Conservative Voters: Trump

Moderate Voters: Trump

Young Voters: Trump

Old Voters: Trump

First-time Voters: Trump

Veterans/Military: Trump

Women: Trump

Men: Trump

High School Grads: Trump

College Grads: Trump

It goes on and on and on like a Journey song.

Granted, there are demographic and psychographic groups Trump did not win, but very few. Rubio did better among post-grad folks. Cruz did better among very conservative voters. But the breadth of Trump's win is staggering. And he did the same thing in New Hampshire. He won all the major demographics and almost all the counties.

Donald Trump has now won New Hampshire and South Carolina by double digits. His chances of winning the nomination are above 80 percent, probably closer to 90 percent.

It's time for Republicans and Republican-leaners to start dealing with the probability that Donald J. Trump will be the party's standard-bearer in 2016.

Since 1996, ordinary Americans have warned the political and corporate elites not to ignore their plight. But the elites didn't listen.

They're listening now.

I bet Donald Trump reads my blog

February 22, 2016, 9:30 p.m.

This post created a lot of confusion. I photoshopped a fake Trump tweet directed at me and my tendency to leave our words. It was supposed to be a joke, but friends of mine were furious at Mr. Trump.

Donald Trump probably reads my blog first thing every day.

Until today, I figured Donald Trump never heard of me. He's never mentioned me in his tweet storms. He's never called me an idiot or a liar during a debate. He's never pointed to one of my many egregious typos and tweeted:

"@whennessy left out the word 'for'.
Confused everyone. Worst blogger in politics. Sad!"

(Trump has 6.35 million followers. I'll send him a small donation if he tweet-storms me. His twitterhood is like a small country!)

In the past two years, I've talked about two broad themes.

In 2014, my big theme was the New Political Dichotomy. In 2015, my big theme was leading with the people we want to help (inspired by Arthur C. Brooks of American Enterprise Institute).

I never thought about Donald Trump when I ruminated on those themes. Donald Trump seems like the antithesis of both. Until you read quotes from interviews with people who voted for him in Iowa, New Hampshire, and South Carolina. Then it smacks you in the head. His voters see America's greatest threat as the idiot political elites who don't listen and don't speak to them.

So it turns out I was 100 percent, totally right in both of those themes. More right than even I thought I was.

Let me do a quick summary of those two years in blogging for you.

2014: The New Political Dichotomy

The old battle lines of American politics have been erased. The battle is no longer Left vs. Right, Liberal (or Progressive) vs. Conservative, Democrat vs. Republican, Statism vs. Liberty, or any other old battle. They're all over.

The new dichotomy is Elites (or Establishment) vs. Plebes (or the Rest of Us).

In this new dichotomy, winners will be those who can let go of the bitterness from the old dichotomy. We might have to work with old enemies because there's a greater common threat. For example, in the old dichotomy, we would simply trash whatever came from the mouths of Bernie Sanders and Elizabeth Warren. In the new dichotomy, we recognize that Sanders and Warren are 100 percent right about many of the problems they identify, but the solutions they offer are horrible. Instead of pretending (lying) that they're wrong about corporations and big banks and crony capitalism, we should say "right on," and offer the free market or liberty solution to the common problem. That's the new dichotomy.

2015: Lead With the People You Intend to Help

This is about message more than substance, because messaging is killing conservatism and liberty. Conservatism, Constitutional integrity, and liberty are all abstract concepts. People who worry about those things respond to those words, but that's only about 19 percent of Americans. That leaves 81 percent rolling their eyes and shaking their heads at us as we defend our dogma. On August 10, I wrote:

> "While the dogma must have its defenders, preaching the dogma guarantees that we remain nothing more than an irritant to the Republican establishment and a godsend to progressives.
> Why? Because most people don't care about our dogma. They care about getting through life the best they can. And it's not their job to figure out how our orthodoxy helps them do that.
> Our job is to translate our principles into broad, moral direction for our country with specific

goals that will make people's lives better. Shouting 'liberty,' repeating historical chants like 'give me liberty or give me death,' doesn't improve anyone's life, even the speaker's (Hennessy, Do You Really Want Your Principles to Win? 2015)."

Ted Cruz talks about abstract concepts, but Ronald Reagan talked more like Trump. Reagan was milder than Trump, but he used language the same way. Here's an example: In Cruz's announcement speech at Liberty University, he mentioned "conservative" or "conservatism" six times. Ronald Reagan never used the term when he announced his run in 1979. Reagan talked to regular people about their lives. We latter-day conservatives chat amongst ourselves about abstract concepts, then we wonder why 81 percent of Americans tune us out.

Donald Trump "Tells It Like It Is"

More accurately, people hear Donald Trump tell it like they want to hear it. Even if they don't agree, people love the fact that he's plainspoken and blunt. As he sees it, the elites who've been running America are stupid, and they're getting their asses handed to them by America's trading partners and enemies. And ordinary, working Americans pay the price for our leaders' stupidity. When he's president, he'll build a wall to keep illegals out, and he'll make Mexico pay for it. He'll be the toughest trade negotiator God ever created, and he'll negotiate deals that will make American companies want to move jobs back to the U.S. of A. Millions and millions of great jobs people can be proud of. He'll build a military so strong and so well trained and so well equipped that nobody will ever even consider messing with us ever again. And he doesn't want people dropping dead in the streets because they couldn't afford a doctor. Terrorists? He'll torture their asses. You have a country, or you don't.

You can't get tastier concrete at Ted Drewes. Not a single abstract principle in the mix. Agree or disagree with his positions or his temperament, the man speaks in words you can chew.

The reason Donald Trump has the broadest and deepest support in the 2016 race is because he speaks in concrete imagery from the perspective of the Plebes in the New Dichotomy. Trump leads with the people he wants to help. There's nothing more concrete than a wall. There's no one who deserves more help than someone who wants to work and can't find a decent job.

And nothing builds loyalty like helping someone help himself.

I'm not saying Trump is a conservative. I'm not saying he'll make a great president. And I'm not saying Trump actually believes everything he says. I really don't know. I am saying he probably reads my blog and decided to put to the test my ideas of a new dichotomy expressed in concrete terms about the people he wants to help.

And so far, the test is working, so I guess I was right. Good for me!

Too bad more candidates don't read me.

David Limbaugh echoes many of my points on messaging, specifically for Ted Cruz. In Suggested Cruz Campaign Reboot: Show, Don't Tell, Limbaugh says:

> "Ted Cruz has everything it takes to be an extraordinary – even historic – president and lead the nation out of its current quagmire.
> "He just needs to say what he's going to do, in concrete terms, and underscore why he can be counted on more than all others to do it – because of his record, his commitment to action and his demonstrated courage in fighting establishment power brokers who will resist him (Limbaugh 2016)."

A crushing defeat for Glenn Beck

February 24, 2016, 12:05 a.m.

How do you feel about Glenn Beck? Is he a patriot or shameless self-promoter?

Glenn Beck was pretty sure that God killed Antonin Scalia so Ted Cruz would win the presidency.

Glenn Beck's theology is very different from mine.

In 2010, I worried that Glenn Beck was doing more harm than good. For days, I'd watched Beck tell his watchers that the world was ending and they would be crushed. Here's what I wrote:

> "Beck offers no solutions. At least, he hasn't in the past two days. Yes, he tells us to pray. But he's unwittingly driving people toward catatonia. And he's doing this to the very people we most need engaged right now (Hennessy, Is Glenn Beck Helping? 2010)."

To be honest, I was pissed at Beck. He was undoing our work on the ground for Ed Martin. Glenn Beck was effectively discouraging people from voting.

Jump ahead to 2016. Glenn Beck, just a few months after announcing his exit from politics and from the Republican party, Beck decided that God is a Cruz guy, and God commanded him to endorse Ted Cruz. And God commanded YOU to vote for Ted Cruz.

Walter Hudson of PJ Media describes the problems with Beck's weird revelation:

> "Glenn Beck has endorsed Ted Cruz for president, which his organization emphasized as his "first ever presidential endorsement." That distinction proves significant in the context of Beck's dominionism. He has said that Cruz was "raised for this hour" by the "hand of divine providence." Most recently, Beck has offered the outlandish claim that God brought about the death of Supreme Court Justice Antonin Scalia to "wake up" conservative voters and summon support for Cruz.
>
> "As a Christian, I retain unshakable faith in the sovereignty of God. In a sense, you could truthfully say that He brought about Scalia's death, but only in the same way that He has brought about anything that has ever happened. Assigning special theological significance to a particular death or a particular candidacy for president requires a certain level of presumption that I, for one, would not dare."

God isn't doing Glenn Beck any favors tonight.

Donald Trump not only blew away expectations for Nevada, but he also registered a record number of new voters in the state. And he broke through the media-imposed glass ceiling of 32 percent. With about 30 percent of the votes counted, Trump has 45 percent! Including more than 40 percent of the Hispanic vote.

In short, Trump became the nominee-apparent tonight.

Trump received 50 percent of the Evangelical vote (according to Fox News entrance polls), almost doubling Ted Cruz's support from that group. Cruz's theory was that Evangelicals would carry him to the White House.

Trump won women, men, Hispanics, and post-grad educated voters. Trump won it all.

Glenn Beck tried to drag God into a political campaign. In the process, he dragged a lot of good people into this race with lies and promises of magic. Now, Beck has been exposed as a charlatan. Let's hope he has the decency to retire to the rock he crawled out from.

How bad would Trump presidency be?

February 24, 2016, 9:45 p.m.

Have you ever predicted something would "ruin my life," only to discover . . . meh?

The world is about to end.

Or civil war is about to break out in Dayton, Ohio.

Believe it?

Glenn Beck, Erick Erickson, and other Republicans have convinced a lot of people that we are doomed if Donald Trump wins the Republican nomination. I know some people who are nearly incapacitated with fear and grief after last night's Nevada caucuses. Because they listen to Glenn Beck. Sad!

Here's the thing: nothing is as bad as you think it will be while you're thinking about it.

I learned that line from a great TED talk by Harvard psychologist Dan Gilbert. It's one of the top 20 TED talks of all time for a reason. Dan is a brilliant guy who studies happiness. In case you never saw the TED talk, here are three big takeaways that will help you tomorrow and for the rest of your life.

> "One year after winning the lottery or losing the use of your legs, you'll be just as happy as you were before the event.
> "These are the data. You failed the pop quiz, and you're hardly five minutes into the lecture. Because the fact is that a year after losing the use of their legs, and a year after winning the lotto, lottery winners and paraplegics are equally happy with their lives (Gilbert 2004)."

We are terrible at predicting how a future event will affect our happiness.

> "From field studies to laboratory studies, we see that winning or losing an election, gaining or losing a romantic partner, getting or not getting a promotion, passing or not passing a college test, on and on, have far less impact, less intensity and much less duration than people expect them to have. This almost floors me – a recent study showing how

major life traumas affect people suggests that if it happened over three months ago, with only a few exceptions, it has no impact whatsoever on your happiness (Gilbert 2004)."

Happiness can be synthesized, and synthesized happiness is often better than organic.

"Why? Because happiness can be synthesized. Sir Thomas Brown wrote in 1642, 'I am the happiest man alive. I have that in me that can convert poverty to riches, adversity to prosperity. I am more invulnerable than Achilles; fortune hath not one place to hit me.' What kind of remarkable machinery does this guy have in his head?

"Well, it turns out it's precisely the same remarkable machinery that all of us have. Human beings have something that we might think of as a 'psychological immune system.' A system of cognitive processes, largely non-conscious cognitive processes, that help them change their views of the world, so that they can feel better about the worlds in which they find themselves. Like Sir Thomas, you have this machine. Unlike Sir Thomas, you seem not to know it (Gilbert 2004)."

Let's go back to November 2012. Remember how you felt after the networks called the election for Obama? And now think back to December 2012. Did you celebrate Christmas? New Years? I'm guessing that between December 2012 and December 2015, you were just about as happy as you were between December 2005 and

December 2008.

Don't make your happiness contingent on an election. It's not worth it. Glenn Beck will not give away his millions and live in a cave if Trump wins. He'll go on saying crazy, insane things that ruin people's days because that's what Glenn Beck does. People pay him to ruin their days. (Stupid me–ruining people's days for free.)

Yes, many people expected the next president would be a constitutional conservative. (I hate that phrase and love the concept.) But what's the worst that could happen?

You think Trump will dissolve Congress and become a dictator? We thought Obama would do that. And, while Obama has overreached his authority as President, so far he's done nothing that can't be undone. The only undoable things that have happened were Supreme Court rulings. And a constitutional amendment can undo those. A change in presidents won't make much of a difference.

You think Ted Cruz would fail to enforce the Supreme Court's gay marriage ruling? How would that be different from Obama refusing to enforce immigration laws? Cruz might not prosecute bakers who won't bake cakes, but he'll recognize same-sex marriages in law. If he doesn't, he doesn't really believe in the rule of law, does he?

So what's the worst that could happen with President Trump? Let's assume that he's serious about the few things he's talked about most:

- He'll build a wall and enforce immigration laws
- He'll suspend Islamic immigration until we "figure out what's going on."
- He'll rebuild the military
- He'll fix the VA
- He'll protect gun rights
- He'll tear up the Iran nuclear deal and craft a new one that works
- He'll demand fair trade practices from China, Mexico, Japan, and other partners
- He'll cut individual taxes on most Americans and simplify the tax code
- He'll cut corporate rates and repatriate trillions of dollars currently off-shore
- He'll repeal Obamacare and replace it with something better

Please tell me if accomplishing those goals would make you happy. Notice I didn't ask if the list is complete, and I didn't ask if you think Trump can do it. (He can, but that's a different matter.) I'm asking you to tell me in the comments if you'd be happy if Trump accomplished all of those things. I know you'll answer truthfully.

Maybe he won't champion pro-life legislation, but it

sounds to me like he'll enforce the law on life. And I suspect he'll sign a pro-life legislation if any comes from Congress. A lot like Reagan. He repeatedly said he would defund Planned Parenthood unless they stop performing abortions. There's no reason to disbelieve him.

He's also talked about eliminating waste in government. Is that a bad thing?

Sure, I like Cruz's tax plan and Carson's tax plan better, but I'll gladly take Trump's. It's a big improvement, and it would make it easier to implement Cruz's later. And Trump told Adam Carolla he likes Cruz's plan a lot better than the status quo. So if Cruz can get Congress to pass his tax plan, Trump will sign it.

Now think about this: would it be any easier for Cruz to get the flat tax through Congress as President? The Kemp-Roth tax package from Reagan's days had a team of dedicated members of Congress working for years to get that overhaul through. Years. If Cruz's plan does not have a coalition to push it now, it won't when he's President.

So the chances of enacting Cruz's tax plan are actually better with Trump in the White House and Cruz working full time in the Senate. No one in Congress can champion Cruz's plan like Senator Cruz can, right?

If you look at Trump's life, it's easy to see him accomplishing most of the goals on his list. I think he can.

He really does have a history of getting stuff done when no one else could figure out how.

Further, I think Trump is probably the most likely of the remaining Republican candidates to win in November. I know what the conventional wisdom says, but the conventional wisdom has been completely wrong about Trump since day one.

The fact is, Cruz's November strategy was tragically flawed. He banked on a groundswell of evangelicals who didn't vote in 2012. But he was wrong. Evangelicals voted in large number in 2012–more than in 2008. The voters who didn't vote in 2012 were working Americans–the very people Trump has fired up. Many of them are also evangelical, but they're not Cruz evangelicals–they're Reagan Democrats and Ross Perot voters. Those record turnouts in Iowa, New Hampshire, South Carolina, and Nevada were largely owing to Trump, not Cruz.

And Rubio's strategy is Romney's strategy warmed-over. With less money. And a less accomplished politician.

If Trump continues to defy conventional expectations through November, he will win in a landslide.

And, again, I ask: with a Republican Congress, how terrible would a President Trump be?

Having read The Art of the Deal, I am confident that Trump is not a globalist and he loves America. He really,

really loves America. While I disagree with a number of his positions, some strongly, I truly believe he'd make a much better president than Hillary or Obama. He might cause some face-palm moments for us, but not because of groveling to a tinhorn dictator.

I'm not telling anyone to abandon your favorite candidate right now. I'm saying think critically about what a President Trump would really be like. I can promise you that it won't be as bad as you think it will be when you're thinking about it–and it might be a whole lot better.

Trump knocks Rubio out of the news cycle

February 26, 2016, 6:42 p.m.

Who understands news cycles better than anyone?

That was a strategic kill shot, to borrow Dilbert cartoonist Scott Adams's word. And it changes everything for conservatives.

After a so-so debate performance and in the middle of a 16-hour verbal assault from Marco Rubio, Trump went nuclear. But not the way everyone would expect Trump to go nuclear.

Trump didn't need to invent a brilliant new put-down line to counter Marco. Instead, he calmly introduced Chris

Christie to 10,000 fans in Texas. Christie did the rest.

> "I am proud to be here to endorse Donald Trump to be president of the United States."

Now that is a kill-shot.

Former RNC chairman Michael Steele told Breitbart News, "One word: BOOM! Exclamation point," about the endorsement:

> "Today after what we saw Marco Rubiodo last night, he was out there attacking Trump on Twitter and Trump was like, got one for you, BOOM! Now the guy who defined Marco a few weeks ago is back in the game. He's engaged, and he's working with Trump. BOOM!"

And New Gingrich tweeted:

> This Chris Christie endorsement of Trump is real signal to GOP establishment that they had better begin thinking about Trump as the future

— Newt Gingrich (@newtgingrich) February 26, 2016

Chris Christie endorsement of Trump is a major breakthrough.this is a huge step for Trump and will impact super tuesday bug time.
— Newt Gingrich (@newtgingrich) February 26, 2016

Just a little while later, Maine's governor endorsed Trump. And John Kasich predicted a Trump sweep on

Super Tuesday, saying "nobody's gonna win but Trump," before admitting he doesn't know about Texas.

Meanwhile, Peggy Noonan offers the best explanation of Trump's rise I've read so far in <u>Trump and the Rise of the Unprotected</u>:

> "There are the protected and the unprotected. The protected make public policy. The unprotected live in it. The unprotected are starting to push back, powerfully.
>
> "The protected are the accomplished, the secure, the successful—those who have power or access to it. They are protected from much of the roughness of the world. More to the point, they are protected from the world they have created. Again, they make public policy and have for some time (Noonan, Trump and the Rise of the Unprotected 2016)."

The "unprotected." Perfect.

Sarah Palin made it okay for Tea Partiers to support Trump. With Christie's endorsement, it's now okay for mainstream Republicans to admit they hate the elites. Trump is a natural leader in the new political dichotomy and the perfect embodiment of the Generation X election.

For conservatives, it's time to stop the fatalism and start planning how to get the best possible policies from the Trump administration.

I'm Trying to Write the Truth

February 27, 2016, 9:30 p.m.

When friends threaten to abandon you over politics, you have to state your case in clear, honest terms, do you not?

I was a pretender.

In 2012, I pretended I believed Mitt Romney would win. But I knew better. I just didn't have the heart to tell the truth to the volunteers banging doors and working call lists from our election office in South County.

But I knew Romney would lose. I suspected the GOP would not regain the Senate.

I could not look at my fellow Tea Partiers at the election night watch party in our South County office. Like a coward, I sat in the back room blogging. Still, I could hear them in the big room, yelling at the TV as one state after another fell to Obama. "You're wrong! They've only counted three percent of the votes!"

After that night, I told myself "never again." I was done encouraging magical thinking. Though I sometimes get the facts wrong, I try to tell the truth when it's important. Which is why you've been reading a lot about Donald Trump on this blog.

In the summer of 2015, I was firmly in the anti-Trump

camp with posts like *Trump: Good, Bad, and Ugly*, We *Deserve Better*, and *Trump: The Final Nail in the Conservative Coffin*? All reproduced earlier in this book.

The fact that most people expected Trump to win told me I should stop writing him off, but in August and September, I still thought he'd fade.

Then came the Islamic terrorist attacks in France and San Bernardino. Those events led me to believe Trump would win. I wasn't happy about it, but my gut said 'it's over."

Starting in December, I did a lot of critical thinking. I challenged my own beliefs about Donald Trump. Some views changed, some were dropped, many survived. In the process, I gained some new beliefs, too. For instance, I learned that Trump is a master of persuasion. Since one of my titles is Persuasive Design Director, I should have recognized this skill sooner. But my professional judgment had been clouded by my personal animosity. Confirmation bias blinded me to many of Trump's qualities.

I wasn't sure how to present my revelation to the world. So I avoided the subject as much as possible. I was afraid writing or speaking the truth as I saw it would anger my friends who still hated Trump or believed Ted Cruz was divinely anointed to be our 45th president. I was afraid that telling the truth would sound like an endorsement to the deep parts of their brains where powerful feelings and emotions lurk. I was afraid I'd be called a "sell-out" just for telling the truth as I saw it. Brave, I know.

Then I started seeing so many people trapped in self-imposed confirmation bias loops, or affinity bubbles. Just like I was last summer. In the conservative echo chamber, Trump became a larger-than-life monster bent on destroying America.

So I decided to write *It's Time to Choose* and *Party Like It's 1992*, also reprinted earlier.

I wasn't trying to change anyone's vote; I wanted to prepare them for what I believed was inevitable. And I was trying to get people to critically examine their beliefs of the likeliest results and most probable consequences of the nomination process. I wanted to caution people against making promises they couldn't keep or predictions they wouldn't want to be repeated.

I particularly wanted Cruz supporters to realize his Evangelical strategy was flawed. It was based on bad interpretation of data from 2012 and 2008. The analysts who came up with the strategy failed to measure all the variables that were available. If they had, they'd have discovered that **the missing voters of 2012 were not conservative Evangelicals**, but Ross Perot voters and Reagan Democrats. Here's what Sean Trende of

RealClearPolitics wrote:

> "What Cruz is really talking about doing is something akin to what Barack Obama did in 2008, when he turned a sizeable number of non-voting African-Americans into voters. Cruz is hoping that evangelicals and conservatives who have traditionally just not voted will opt to vote for him. It's a tough haul, since the National Election Study suggests turnout among born-again Christians is around 80 percent to begin with. But stranger things have happened (I suppose).
>
> "The candidate who actually fits the profile of a 'missing white voter' candidate is Donald Trump. As I noted Wednesday, he fits in the mold of the Nixon-Perot-Huckabee-Santorum populist strain of Republicanism (Trende, Cruz, Trump, and the Missing White Voter 2016)."

In other words, Cruz's plan was to get his top-performing segment to perform even better. Every motivation designer knows that's very difficult and very expensive and runs the risk of frustrating your best supporters. (Remember, I do persuasion and motivation for a living.)

At this point I had three strong data points suggesting Trump would probably win the nomination:

Trump has remarkable persuasion skills (Adams, Updating the Persuasion Stack (National Review's Trump Cover) 2016).

Voters expected Trump to win, and voter expectations

are far more accurate at predicting winners than voter preference polls (because voters lie).

Cruz's Evangelical strategy was flawed, but Donald Trump was designed for the "missing white voter."

So when *National Review*, Glenn Beck, and others lost their minds in December 2015 and January 2016, I felt I had to step up my game. They were actually helping Trump, not hurting him.

Since then, Trump has won three straight primaries and caucuses, and he's expected to sweep or nearly sweep Super Tuesday. He picked up two endorsements from sitting governors, and Newt Gingrich now believes the nomination is over.

Some readers might think it's my fault for not doing more for Cruz. Well, Cruz was never my first choice. I like all of his policies, but that's not enough. Cruz's policies are not popular with Congressional Republicans. Congress will not rubber-stamp whatever a President Cruz sends up the hill. (If he couldn't get the bills through the Senate as a Senator, why would he be able to do it as President?) To be effective, a president must be persuasive. If Ted Cruz can't persuade a majority of Evangelicals to vote for him in South Carolina or Nevada, how will he persuade Congress to pass his flat tax? But, most of all, I never saw a path to the White House for Cruz. His general election strategy was too flawed, as I've said many times already.

I am not trying to influence the election. I'm just trying to tell people what I think will happen. And I'm encouraging people to have a useful contingency plan in case I'm right. I do this knowing you might not want to hear it from me. But I know that hearing it early will make the realization less painful.

I've learned that writing the truth is a lot harder than encouraging people's fantasies. It hurts me to know my honesty pains some readers, but I think it's my job as a blogger. And if the truth as I see it is too painful, you don't have to read my posts. But I'm glad you do.

Thanks for reading.

The Psychology of The Inevitable

May 1, 2016, 11:58 p.m.

Between February and May, I took a break from blogging to allow a sort of peace to settle in. I believed in February the race was essentially over, but my posts were causing a lot of pain to people I love and admire. I returned to the keyboard when I sensed everyone knew what was about to happen.

I have no idea who will win the Indiana primary 72 hours from the time I write. But the people inside Ted Cruz's campaign seem to have an idea. And it's not good for them. Cruz's top team expects their candidate to lose. And Senator Cruz seems to have accepted that outcome.

Expectations Matter More Than Preferences

Regular readers know that polls that ask "who do you think will win" trump polls that ask "who do you intend to vote for" or even "who did you vote for?"

Social psychologists and pollsters give several reasons for this, but the one that seems most likely is sample size. When I think about who will win, I do a quick mental poll of the people I know and how they intend to vote. Late in 2015, I realized that most of my friends said they were voting for Trump. As noted earlier, expectations are more accurate than preference polls in predicting outcomes of elections.

On August 24, 2015, I came across a poll: 57 percent of Republicans then expected Trump to become the nominee. It's possible that the whole nominating process was already finished last August. If race wasn't over then, it's over now.

Slouching Toward Indiana

Inevitability has crept into Ted Cruz's mind, too. He's behaving like a man who knows he's lost. I watched his rally speech in Jeffersonville, Indiana, last Friday, just four days before the Indiana primary. Cruz's demeanor and even his words reminded me of Senator Marco Rubio's speeches in the days before the Florida primary. The anger was gone. The energy was there, but it was a different kind of energy. In Jeffersonville, Cruz showed the sort of energy we see in a man who shrugged a great weight off his shoulders. The word "acceptance" comes to mind.

If Trump wins Indiana on Tuesday, expect Cruz to speak early, thank his supporters, congratulate Donald Trump, and set the stage for the next act in his political career. Just like Marco Rubio the evening of the Florida primary.

As explained in this Politico story, Inside the Cruz Campaign, Confidence Crumbles:

> "Within the campaign, some are turning to the question of what's next. One senior aide said there had been no discussion about dropping out before the final primary contests are held on June 7 but noted that Cruz wouldn't be eager to prolong a campaign he was convinced he couldn't win (Isenstadt 2016)."

I realize that strong Cruz supporters will see his Jeffersonville performance differently. That's okay. They're supposed to keep the faith. The most likely outcome–almost inevitable at this point–is that Donald Trump will leave Indiana without a major opponent to the nomination.

Yes, I've seen the reports that Cruz intends to continue his campaign even if he loses Indiana. But before Florida, Rubio said he'd continue on even if he lost his home state.

To detect a difference in Cruz's demeanor, I compared two speeches. One from Iowa just a week before the Iowa caucuses. The other from Jeffersonville, Indiana, the Friday before the Indiana primary. I looked for tone, volume, tempo, body language, and facial expression. I also looked at language.

In Iowa, Cruz was fired up and combative. In Indiana, Cruz was almost apologetic at first, in the theological sense of the word. He was explaining his campaign rather than prosecuting it. Again, the polls could be wrong. But Cruz seems to believe the polls showing Trump in charge in the Hoosier state correct. A CNN source revealed those Cruz internal numbers:

> "But earlier in the week, Cruz allies and people close to the campaign described a budding sense of gloom, with internal polls diving as Trump mounted even stronger than expected showings in his native northeast. In Indiana, which Cruz backers once believed they were favored to win after his strong defeat of Trump in Wisconsin, Cruz's numbers have fallen precipitously: Once leading, Cruz now trails in the state by eight8 to 10 points, according to a person who has seen the numbers, with Trump over the 40% mark. Cruz's campaign did not respond when asked about those figures (Schleifer and Bradner 2016)."

Remember the fish study. People want to go with the winner.

We See What We Want to See

Of course, Trump haters and Cruz lovers will see things a little different. What I saw in Iowa was a man on the ascent, fairly confident of victory. In Indiana, I saw a man who has accepted defeat but soldiers on to fulfill a commitment to his supporters. In between, Cruz passed through several stages of grief, including denial and anger. But that anger has gone away now.

Senator Cruz probably knows what I know, that expectation polls trump preference polls. And the latest poll of Republican expectations came out on Friday. Here's how Rasmussen described the results:

> "Belief that Donald Trump is the likely Republican presidential nominee has soared to its highest level ever and matches perceptions that Hillary Clinton will be the Democratic standard-bearer in the fall.
>
> "The latest Rasmussen Reports weekly Trump Change survey, taken following Trump's five state primary wins on Tuesday, finds that 89% of Likely Republican Voters now think the billionaire businessman is likely to win the GOP nomination. Two-out-of-three (67%) say Trump's nomination is Very Likely, up 18 points from 49% last week and up from 38% two weeks ago before Trump's fortunes turned around with his mega-win in New

York State (Rasmussen Reports 2016)."

It's still possible, of course, that Trump could stumble, but he'll have to fall fast and hard to lose the nomination. Cruz knows this and indicated on Friday that his campaign is dead if he loses badly in Indiana. And the latest Wall Street Journal/NBC News poll shows that the Cruz internal numbers were right: Trump is surging in Indiana (Hook 2016) (Hook 2016). Via WSJ.com:

> "Donald Trump holds a 15-point lead in the Republican presidential primary in Indiana, and a majority of GOP voters disapprove of the effort by underdogs in Indiana. And the latest Wall Street Journal/NBC News poll shows that the Cruz internal numbers were right: Tt Poll finds."

For the record, I have not endorsed Donald Trump or any of the candidates still campaigning. (I supported Ben Carson.) I have warned that Trump is not a conservative, but I've also pointed out that a Trump presidency probably won't be as bad as many people think. And I prefer Trump to any Democrat because Trump will likely appoint more reasonable federal judges and Supreme Court justices. You know how important the courts are.

Time to Start on Hillary

When asked about national head-to-head polls against

Hillary Clinton, Donald Trump likes to say, "I haven't even started on her yet."

It's time. Everyone expects Trump to be the Republican nominee, and expectations matter.

The good news: the civil war on the right probably ends Tuesday when Senator Cruz suspends his campaign. Better news: if Senator Cruz can get his new friends in the US Senate to pass some of the legislation he's campaigned on, President Trump will sign it.

Finally, I'm a strategist, not a pollster. I am less concerned with what will happen than what people should do about what happens. If Cruz loses Indiana, the best outcome would be for Cruz to suspend his campaign and focus on influencing his fellow Senators to send great legislation to President Trump's desk in 2017. On the other hand, Cruz could win Indiana in a landslide and make me look like a terrible forecaster.

For Trump

May 3, 2016, 11:59 p.m.

Oddly enough, I was in Indianapolis on the evening of the Indiana Primary. This post was my immediate reaction to Ted Cruz's announcement that he was suspending his campaign.

I'm for Trump.

I like stating the positive.

So I'm for Trump.

The *National Review* Against Trump writers can own it if Hillary wins and appoints a Supreme Court justice who's to the left of Bader-Ginsberg as Scalia's replacement. They'll take that to their graves.

For me, I'm for Trump. I'll admit he wasn't my first choice, but he was far from my last choice. My first choice, Ben Carson, endorsed The Donald.

Trump seems to love America and Americans. His kids love him. His ex-wife endorsed him. And he has a history of accomplishing things everybody else thought hopeless.

A lot of people think America is hopeless, but Trump thinks he can fix it. Why not give him this chance? No one else has a plausible plan to fix our country. Trump's plan might be a little vague, but it's still viable. Everybody else's plan was dead on arrival. And who doesn't want to make America great again? Reagan did.

So I'm for Trump. How bad could it be?

I'm working on a longer post. Look for it on Sunday. But this one pretty much sums up my feelings and thoughts tonight, the night Americans rejected the political elite and took a chance on someone different from anything we've seen before.

I'm for America.

I'm for Trump.

An Affair to Dismember (Trump)

May 4, 2016, 5:28 p.m.

What is the cost of opposing Trump in November?

If you've ever cheated on your spouse just to get back at your daughter for marrying the wrong man, you're probably a #nevertrump person like George Will.

Suppose your daughter married a man you didn't approve of. You would probably respond by cheating on your own spouse, would you not? Having an affair would teach your daughter a lesson, right? And if your spouse and your friends and your other children suffered, too bad. Collateral damage is the cost of war.

Because Republican voters nominated a candidate the NeverTrumpers disapprove of, the NeverTrumpers say they'll politically sleep with a woman who intentionally built an email server to hide her Clinton Foundation money-laundering operation from law enforcement. For example, NeverTrumper and conservative blogger George Will plans to have an affair with Hillary Clinton, the woman who pressured Obama to turn Libya into an ISIS breeding ground. Hillary Clinton, who publicly blamed the Benghazi attack on a video even after her illegal emails revealed she knew damn well it was an act of terrorism. Then she called the families of Benghazi victims liars. George Will will sleep with Hillary Clinton who promised to put "a lot of coal miners and a lot of coal companies out of business," then told an out-of-work coal miner he didn't hear what she said.

And George Will wants to sleep with this woman. Politically speaking, of course.

I realize George is an old man. He was old in 2009 when he warned that blue jeans would lead to the downfall of Western Civilization. Will wrote, "it is a straight line from the fall of the Bastille to the rise of denim." In the same post, Mr. Will prescribed a model of male dress that, in his view, should guide every man from here to eternity: "If Fred Astaire would not have worn it, don't wear it (Will 2009)." (The 90 percent of you who have no idea who Fred Astaire was can look him up on Wikipedia. I guess.) That "jeans are devil-wear" column was the moment level-headed people stopped taking Will seriously.

On Monday, lead NeverTrumper Bill Kristol said he'll "never say never" about voting for Trump after having said "never Trump" about two million times. Kristol's wisdom to walk back his never Trump statements will shine through as Donald Trump goes to work on Hillary Clinton.

Benghazi and the emails will, finally, became household scandals. People old enough to remember the 1990s will sober up and realize the horrific danger to America Hillary presents.

Those Republicans who insist on sleeping with Hillary? Wear a condom. You don't want to get any on you.

I'm for America. I'm for Trump.

World Leaders and Paul Ryan Begin Negotiating With Trump

May 5, 2016, 9:31 p.m.

Common knowledge is what everyone knows everyone else knows. And people act on common knowledge.

Every prediction about Trump has been wrong. Except for two. Ann Coulter and Scott Adams predicted Trump would win the nomination and, eventually, the White House in a landslide. They were right.

World leaders expect Trump to win, and they are lining up to make all his crazy assertions look like brilliant predictions.

Former Mexico President Vicente Fox apologized to Trump, and Trump graciously accepted. That's a sign that Mexicans expect Trump to become the next US president.

China's leaders urged everyone to treat Trump "with objectivity." That's a big change from just a few weeks ago when China was calling Trump names. China's afraid of Trump, and they want a fair deal from his administration. They know the days of conning American negotiators are coming to an end.

British Prime Minister David Cameron admitted his "respect" for Donald Trump. David Cameron realizes he'll need Trump's spine to keep England from falling to radical Islamists.

And House Speaker Paul Ryan demonstrated his respect for Trump by opening negotiations for a spot in Trump's cabinet. Ryan's opening position was brilliant. By saying he's not yet ready to endorse Trump, Ryan signaled to the master negotiator that Ryan knows how to deal. Trump earned a lot of respect for Ryan. That's why Trump responded with an official release saying that Trump is not ready to endorse Ryan's agenda. Negotiation students better keep an eye on this exchange. These two guys are about the top two negotiators on the planet, and Ryan will probably end up with the cabinet post of his choice.

This process will play out over the coming months. The leaders who've dissed and trashed Trump, now expecting him to win the White House, will join the negotiations Trump started last June. Those leaders with no leverage will simply fold the way Vicente Fox did. Those with some leverage will stake out a strong position like Paul Ryan. Not right away, but soon, all of Trump's "enemies" will be negotiating with The Donald through the media.

In other words, everyone who doubted Trump's ability to win great deals for America will watch him practice his art on Twitter and TV. You'll love this. You'll want to help make America great again, won't you?

For the record, now that he is the only viable alternative to Hillary Clinton, I'm for Trump. And the NeverTrumpers are having an affair to get back at their daughters.

Trump for President. I Endorse.

May 6, 2016, 1:05 p.m.

Some people accused me of hedging my support for Donald Trump after my May 3 "For Trump" post. I decided to remove all doubt.

> You can choose a ready guide in some celestial voice
> If you choose not to decide, you still have made a choice
> You can choose from phantom fears and kindness that can kill
> I will choose a path that's clear
> I will choose freewill
> –RUSH, *Freewill*

Last July and August and once in September, I was down on Donald Trump. I predicted that a Trump nomination would be the final nail in the coffin of conservatism.

I was right. The brilliant Ed Morrissey agrees.

But I was wrong, too. I totally underestimated Donald Trump.

I read (scanned?) The Art of the Deal back in the 1990s. Had I read it carefully, I might not have made that error last July. Or I might have. I don't know.

But I re-read The Art of the Deal recently and realized something amazing: Donald Trump gets things done. More importantly, Donald Trump gets things done that everyone thought couldn't be done.

The Commodore Hotel.

Central Park Ice Rink.

Trump Tower.

Trump Taj Mahal.

The smartest executives in the industries involved said all of those magnificent projects could not possibly be completed.

Trump completed them.

Under budget

On time.

Trump gets things done.

And now he's getting this election done.

Hillary should run in fear.

Earlier I mentioned Ed Morrissey. Now I'm going to share with you something Ed wrote. Something you should memorize.

> "Conservatism has to be more than a debating society. It has to offer practical improvements, and in order to do that, it has to engage people where they live. For too long, the conservative movement has mainly argued philosophy and employed obstructionism while assuming the rest of country understood the stakes. As this primary has demonstrated, even many self-identified conservatives have tired of ideology and all-or-nothing politics.
>
> "Until the conservative movement rolls up its sleeves and does the hard work of engaging voters and applying solutions rather than slogans, the reaction from voters they desperately need will continue to be, 'Who cares? We have to straighten out the country (Morrissey 2016).'"

Holy crap! That's it! That's why I don't call myself a conservative any longer. Conservatism has no meaning.

So many members of the conservative debate society. Do they give a crap about anybody's real life problems? Sad. They can't win votes. They hate America if America stands in the way of their narrow, shallow, weak visions. Sad

I want America to be GREAT again.

I want my boys, who serve our country in the US Navy, to come home alive.

I want a military so huge that it deters aggression.

I want two decades *without* a war.

I want a vibrant economy.

I want men to be men.

I want women to feel safe.

I want a civil society.

I want to speak my mind.

I want my grandchildren to believe life only gets better.

I want good jobs for people who don't have advanced degrees.

I want America to be great again.

Therefore, I endorse Donald J. Trump for President of the United States. Because he's the only sonofabitch in this race who wants those things to happen.

For America. For Trump.

Who Is Conservative?

May 8, 2016, 5:49 p.m.

Trump lacks Reagan's gentle optimism, but how different are they on policy?

People think they're rational, but we're not. For example, on many issues, Trump's positions are almost identical to Ronald Reagan's. When it comes to abortion, trade, taxes, foreign policy and the military, and entitlements like Social Security, you can't fit a dime between Reagan and Trump.

So why do people see Trump as far to the left of Reagan? Contrasts and comparisons.

Reagan ran against George Bush and John B. Anderson. Also-rans included Howard Baker and Phil Crane, John Connally, Harold Stassen, Bob Dole, Larry Pressler, and Lowell Weicker. That made Reagan the most conservative Republican by a wide margin. George H. W. Bush was an eastern seaboard Rockefeller Republican in 1979 and 1980. Bush didn't become a conservative until after he became Reagan's VP. John B. Anderson never became a conservative. Anderson ran as an independent to try to throw the election to Jimmy Carter. Bill Kristol is a lot like John Anderson. And in four years, Kristol will be forgotten just like Anderson.

Conservative is relative. I know conservatives tend to believe there's no such thing as relativity, but they're wrong about that. Conservatism is relative. I won't bother with defining left-right or liberal-conservative or any other dimensions of political thought. They're meaningless. But I will point out that all of the definitions I've seen are relative. A position is conservative or liberal only relative to other positions.

Nowhere does the constitution mention "conservatism." And the modern concept of conservatism didn't really exist at the time of our founding. America's founders were pretty much all radical liberals for their time. They believed in liberty, and they were willing to overthrow their government to get it. That's very radical and very liberal.

I think modern conservatism seeks to conserve classical liberalism. But that's just my opinion. You are entitled to be as mistaken as me.

But let's play pretend for a moment that there is a conservative absolute. If there were, Ronald Reagan would be the only absolute conservative president in the lifetimes of anyone now alive, would he not? Everyone agrees.

So let's see how Trump compares to Reagan on some key issues and themes, okay?

Issue	Trump	Reagan
Theme	Make America Great Again	Let's Make America Great Again
Trade	45% tariff on unfair imports from China	100% tariff on Japanese semi-conductors, 45% tariff on Japanese motorcycles
Abortion	Opposes abortion except cases of rape, incest, or life of mother	Opposed abortion except to save the life of the mother
Social Security	Committed to preserving Social Security, eliminate fraud and waste, increase efficiency	…ironclad commitment to Social Security, signed 1983 bill and encouraged every Republican to read it. "To be sure, we must reform it, root out the fraud, make it more efficient, and ensure that the program is solvent."
Taxes	Cut taxes, overhaul tax code, flatten brackets	25% tax cut early, then overhaul tax system & reduce rates
Defense	Build a military so powerful no one will dare bother us, avoid nation-building and open-ended wars of intervention	Rebuilt the military and launched SSD to break the Soviet Union without a war
Illegal Immigration	Build a wall, deport illegal aliens	Granted amnesty to illegal aliens and reform immigration laws

Those are not the only issues, I realize, but they're some of the leading issues of both Reagan and Trump. On some issues, Trump is slightly to Reagan's left. On other issues, like illegal immigration, Trump is somewhat to Reagan's right. Overall, there's little difference between Reagan and Trump on many key issues.

Why does it feel like Trump is so far to Reagan's left? Because memories are fluid. Memories are not fixed. They change over time.

When Reagan took office, we had very few conservative think tanks, few conservative magazines, and a handful of conservative pundits. Since then, conservatism has bloomed into an industry, Conservative, Inc. Tens of thousands of people make their living being conservative. That's something new. And it's made conservatism kind of weird. In fact, Conservative, Inc., has done for conservatism what the Civil Rights Industry has done for African-Americans. That's not a compliment to either corporation. Have you looked at African-American unemployment lately?

Plus, the internet came along after Reagan. The internet lets us all hide inside affinity bubbles–safe spaces where we can hide away from any ideas that we don't agree with. In these affinity bubbles, we morph our memories to fit a narrative. We've made Reagan more "conservative" than he was. We've created Reagan in our own image and likeness.

That's why so many Cruz fans lost their minds when Phyllis Schlafly endorsed Trump. A lot of Cruz supporters remember the Reagan years differently than they actually happened. That's just the way the brain works.

I believe the Constitution, though flawed, provides the best government ever conceived for human flourishing. And I believe the best hope for Constitutional government lies in understanding how things really are and dealing with reality on reality's terms. That's why I formally endorsed Donald J. Trump for President.

If you can't vote for Trump because he's too liberal, you probably couldn't have voted for Reagan, either. You just don't remember.

And if you're thinking about voting for Hillary or working against Trump, you'd probably cheat on your wife to punish your daughter for marrying a guy you don't like.

Trump Is the Only Viable Pro-Life Choice

May 9, 2016, 4:30 p.m.

General George Patton said, "A leader adapts principles to circumstances."

Some pro-life activists like Erick Erickson are plotting ways to sabotage Donald Trump's candidacy for president. They probably haven't stopped to think. If they succeed in defeating Trump, they will be culpable in many, many abortions. That's a lot of guilt for a guy like Erickson to carry around, isn't it?

Chances are Congress won't introduce any major abortion laws in the next four years. That means the abortion battle will remain in the courts.

The Supreme Court is made up of four relatively conservative justices and four relatively liberal ones. That means there's a vacancy on the court. Antonin Scalia died in February, leaving an open seat. Scalia was probably the most conservative justice. President Obama appointed a replacement for Scalia, but the Senate probably won't vote on that nomination.

That means the next president will appoint Scalia's replacement, and that appointment will decide whether the court goes mostly right or mostly left.

Now, we can't say for sure whether the GOP or Democrats will control the next Senate. But we can accurately predict this: if Clinton is the next president, the Supreme Court will be mostly liberal for a generation.

Clinton is a big fan of abortion on demand, and she's vowed to appoint judges and justices who will overrule state and federal laws that restrict abortions. I know Hillary lies a lot, but I bet she's telling the truth about this.

Donald Trump says he's working with the Heritage

Foundation to create a list of excellent conservative jurists to replace Scalia and any other vacancies that occur during his presidency. He's even open to appointing Ted Cruz to the Supreme Court. That probably means a Trump win keeps the high court mostly conservative.

I have no way of knowing how many more abortions will happen if Clinton wins, but I'm pretty confident in predicting that a Clinton win means more unborn babies will die than if Trump wins.

If you're pro-life, the choice is pretty simple: support Trump or the baby gets it.

Here's How the Ryan-Trump Meeting Ends

May 11, 2016, 9:28 a.m.

Just showing off some prediction skills.

Nothing happens in politics by accident. Every move has an angle. Some players are better than others. Paul Ryan and Donald Trump are two of the best players alive, but one is better than the other. We'll see that tomorrow.

House Speaker Paul Ryan has set aside Thursday for meetings with his party's nominee for President. Every candidate for president meets with the senior members of his party's Congressional caucus, so there's nothing odd about the meeting. What makes this nominee-speaker meeting different from all other nominee-speaker meetings is this: Ryan has not endorsed his party's nominee.

I wrote previously that **Ryan used his endorsement as leverage**. Donald Trump loves negotiation, so he respects people who know what they're doing. When Ryan said he's not yet ready to endorse, he told Trump, "I know how to negotiate, and I'm ready." Trump responded by saying he's not ready to endorse the speaker's agenda. That's negotiation language for "I received your request to negotiate. My people will get with your people and something will be arranged."

That "something" is a day of meetings.

Here's what's likely to happen:

Ryan will tell Trump all the things that Trump must do to win Ryan's endorsement

Trump will say, "that's not gonna happen, but here's what I'll do if you don't endorse

me."

Ryan will repeat his demands, leaving off two or three

Trump will say, "I'm wasting my time here. See you in Cleveland"

As Trump gets up to leave, Ryan will ask to speak The Donald alone

The lieutenants will trade concerned glances before leaving the room

Alone now with Trump, Ryan will reveal his *real* desire– his actual single "reserve price"

Trump will promise to think about it

Ryan will say, "without that, no endorsement"

Trump will say, "I guess that's the way it is then"

The two will call their lieutenants back in to draft a very friendly joint press release saying "Both the Speaker and Mr. Trump are committed to uniting the Republican Party to defeat Hillary Clinton in November."

At that point, Trump will have won. A joint statement promising to work together to defeat Clinton is as good as an endorsement to the voter's mind. The House leaders who've said they're not ready to endorse Trump will parrot the press release. They'll also pose for photos with Donald Trump, which they'll email to their constituents, explaining how lucky their constituents are to be represented by someone who holds their own party's nominee accountable while *still* looking great in a selfie with him.

Or it could go a completely different way, but it'll end up with all the GOP leadership working to defeat the Democrats in the fall. Which is all anybody wants.

Trump wins.

How to Predict Trump's Landslide Win

May 13, 2016, 3:15 p.m.

Have you made a prediction?

You might have noticed that my predictions have been remarkably accurate lately, have you not?

For example, on Sunday, May 1, I predicted Ted Cruz would suspend his campaign after getting trounced in Indiana. Two days later, Cruz lost the Indiana primary to Donald Trump 53 to 36. At the time I wrote, many pundits and pollster still believed Cruz could win that Indiana race, and everyone believed Cruz was telling the truth when he repeatedly said he was staying in the race to Cleveland unless Trump reached 1,237 delegates before then. Turns out, those pundits were wrong, and I was right. Cruz quit long before Trump won the magic number.

Then on Wednesday morning I predicted Paul Ryan and Donald Trump would end their meeting with a joint statement committing to work together to win in November. Pundits thought Ryan would use the meeting to chastise Trump and drive a permanent wedge between the two men. But the meeting ended with a joint statement that expressed precisely the intention and commitment I forecast.

You might think an ancient Sumerian God speaks to me through my dog Stella. Maybe. But more likely, I've been applying my day-job thinking in human behavior and persuasive design to my forecasting in politics. And it seems to work. While I'm not nearly as good at this as Scott Adams, I'm getting better.

I now predict that you would like to know my secrets for predicting outcomes. Great. I'll tell you. In a moment.

Before that, let me tell you I have no idea if I'm right about any of this. I know just enough psychology to know that people are terrible at understanding their own motivations and errors. For example, psychologists will produce better research papers if they're offered virtual badges for transparency and completeness. If psychologists with PhDs fall for meaningless rewards, I'm pretty sure I have some blind spots, too.

Now, my secrets.

Focus on Words, Voice, Face, and Body

First, I try to focus on individuals. I can learn more about famous people like Ted Cruz and Paul Ryan than I can about millions of people whose names I don't know. Over time, I might be able to accurately predict how many people respond to a given situation. An election, for example. But for now, I'm focusing on these people with a large body of public information. I pay attention to the words they use, their tone, tempo, and volume of voice, their facial expressions, and their body language. These four behaviors–language, voice, face, and body–told me Ted Cruz was a beaten man the Friday before the Indiana primary. Maybe he told no one, but Cruz's brain had already decided his race would end the following Tuesday. No matter how hard he tried, he could not hide what his brain had decided as he spoke to supporters in Jeffersonville, Indiana. The key is to watch people without judging or expecting anything.

Compare to a Baseline

In predicting the Cruz announcement, I had a baseline to compare against. That baseline was Cruz's speech to supporters in Iowa just before the Iowa caucuses. When you watch the two speeches side-by-side, it's impossible to miss the changes in Cruz's words, voice, face, and body. One of the strongest tells was words. In Iowa, Cruz talked about the future, but in Indiana, Cruz spoke almost completely in past tense, saying things like "we ran." The difference in tense was probably entirely subconscious, but it was distinct.

An example of subconscious language tells of future behavior happens when employees are ready to quit their jobs. Employees who've had enough start referring to the company they work for as "it," "they," or "them." Happy employees say "we" and "us." Again, it helps to have a baseline. Some people never refer to the company they work for as "us." But most do–until they're ready to quit.

Consider Their End Games and Interests

Everything in life is a form of negotiation, and most people open negotiations by stating their positions. But, in the end, rational people abandon their positions and, instead, focus on their interests. Crazy people sometimes sacrifice their interests for their positions, but that's always a losing strategy. The cliché that describes choosing position over interest is cutting off one's nose to spite one's face. See #NeverTrump for more examples of people who abandon interests for positions.

Paul Ryan's interest is remaining Speaker of the House. Ryan also wants to get some legislation passed by the Senate and signed by the President. His interests are better served with President Trump than with a Democrat in the White House. I realize NeverTrumpers can't get this through their heads, but a Trump victory in November increases the likelihood of the GOP keeping the House and keeping the Senate. Plus, while Trump's policies are somewhat vague, Clinton's are not. Clinton would veto every bill Republicans like. A Clinton administration would look a lot like Obama's administration when it comes to legislation and compromise. So Ryan's interest is to get Trump elected in November.

Remember that People Decide Emotionally and Defend with Reason

There is no such thing as a rational decision. Zero. All human decisions are emotional. The most important decision most people make is whom to marry. If you think that's a purely rational decision, tell your wife. Then duck. If the most important decision in your life is an emotional decision, the less important decisions are even more emotional. It's obvious.

Children with brain damage that prevents them from connecting to the emotional centers of the brain cannot choose between a black pen and a blue-black pen. There's no rational reason to prefer one over the other, so the kids in the experiment had no information available about which pen to choose. So, even the choice of very dark blue ink or black ink is purely emotional. Understanding that we decide emotionally allowed me to see that Cruz had already decided to leave the race if he lost Indiana. It was that simple.

Reason and facts do matter but only after the decision. For people to remain committed to their decisions, they need rational evidence to defend their decision. It helps to provide facts before people make their decision because the easy availability of these facts makes it easier for people to commit to their emotional decisions. Every salesperson knows this.

Be Bold and Announce What You See

The last step is important and it's the most difficult. To get credit for predictions, you have to announce them. That means you have to be okay with being wrong. Some people would rather die than be wrong, so I don't know what to tell you if you think people decide rationally. I don't want you to die. For you, being wrong in public is very painful, so you probably need to keep your opinions to yourself. I am used to being wrong, so I find it easier to announce my predictions in public.

And that's all there is to my effortless and easy formula for predicting that Cruz would quit the race and that Trump and Ryan would work together to defeat crooked Hillary Clinton and down-ballot Democrats this year. I looked at the behavior of key players, determined their interests, and remembered that they decide emotionally and defend rationally. Then I wrote about it.

Expect Trump to Win in a Landslide

Now I'm pretty sure Trump will win in a landslide in November with about 400 electoral votes. Maybe more, but 400 seems about right. That means he'll win about 40 states. I don't know which 40, but that doesn't matter. If Trump wins 40 states, he'll win about 400 electoral votes. Everyone will call it Trump's Landslide, and Ted Cruz and Paul Ryan will be very happy because President Trump will support and sign their favorite bills. Most people expect Trump to beat crooked Hillary. I know pollsters aren't releasing their expectation polls yet, because those polls would be a disaster for crooked Hillary. But people keep talking about "when Trump's President" and "President Trump." Even crooked Hillary released a "President Trump" video. These are psychological tells, just like Cruz's "we ran." Subconsciously, most people expect Trump to beat crooked Hillary Clinton (assuming she's even allowed to run), and expectations trump preferences.

My only hesitation in making this prediction is that NeverTrumper Glenn Beck also thinks Trump will in November. And Beck is usually wrong, but not always. So predicting the same thing Glenn Beck predicts scares me a little. Still, this time, I'm going to agree with Glenn Beck and stick with what I see: A Trump landslide.

If you think "Never Trump," you must also think "Never Cruz policies" and "Never Ryan policies." That's also called cutting off your nose to spite your face. And that's crazy, folks. That's crazy.

AFTERWORD

If you read this far, you're probably worried about America's future. Everyone who reads a book like this one is concerned with the state of our nation. And the more you read our current situation, the more worried you become, right?

Worrying about your country's direction is natural and healthy. I worry more about the people who never even thinking about the country's track. They will end up where others decide to take them. You, on the other hand, want some control over your life and the life of our country. You probably feel better already now, don't you?

Everyone knows that constitutionally limited government means a lot to me. I helped found a movement dedicated to advancing limited government, fiscal responsibility, and peace through overwhelming strength. Those are, to me and probably to you, the best end goals for a nation.

But they are not enough.

A ruling class has installed itself as the final judges of all things American. You see this in politics, art, education, and even everyday language, do you not? Think of all the little rules that have been handed down to you in the past 20 years. Rules like what words you're allowed to use and who may or may not use your bathroom. Rules like Common Core in your children's school, and rules that prohibit any discussion of Islamic terrorism on Facebook.

This ruling elite is not just government. It's the big media, it's big social networking, education, and even some religions. It's big business, especially the huge mega-banks that control both your checking account and your retirement plan.

In short, we have reduced competition and put all our power into a tiny few hands of "experts" who, we are told, know best. And those experts have screwed up almost everything they've touched. And they punish us when we offer to take control, again, over our own lives.

Until we regain some of that control and diversify the power centers, our society will continue become more fragile, more subject to massive upheavals in financial markets. And until we regain control of our language and our lives, the ruling class will continue to dilute our culture, the culture that allowed ordinary people like you and me to create the American Exception.

As I close out this book, our brave brothers and sisters in the United Kingdom have just rejected the European ruling class. The Brits showed the same courage and conviction on the Brexit vote as our founders showed when they signed the Declaration of Independence in 1776.

I am for Trump, now, because it's time to reject our ruling class and to take control of our nation's destiny. I see no alternative to Trump.

I try to judge every decision on one question: Will it liberate?

Will it liberate?

WORKS CITED

Adams, Scott. 2015. *Trump's Third Act*. October 20. Accessed May 21, 2016. http://blog.dilbert.com/post/131552504961/trumps-third-act-part-of-the-trump-persuasion.

—. 2016. *Updating the Persuasion Stack (National Review's Trump Cover)*. January 22. Accessed May 21, 2016. http://blog.dilbert.com/post/137816083466/updating-the-persuasion-stack-national-reviews.

Bradley, David. 2013. *Casting a shadow over green light bulbs*. January 13. Accessed May 21, 2016. http://www.rsc.org/chemistryworld/2013/01/cfl-led-incandescent-analysis-environment-toxic-metal.

Brooks, Arthur C. 2015. *The Conservative Heart: How to build a fairer, happier, and more prosperous America*. New York: Broadside Books.

Buchanan, Patrick J. 2016. *Is the New Era Upon Us?* February 1. Accessed May 21, 2016. http://buchanan.org/blog/is-a-new-era-upon-us-124686#?1#?1#WebrootPlugIn#?1#?1#PhreshPhish#?1#?1#agtpwd.

—. 2015. *Will Elites Blow Up the GOP?* December 14. Accessed May 21, 2016. http://buchanan.org/blog/will-elites-blow-up-the-gop-124423.

Buckley, William F. Jr. 1988. "Did You Ever See a Dream Walking?" In *Keeping the Tablets: Modern American*

Conservative Thought, by William F. Buckley Jr. and Charles R. Kessler. New York: Perennial Library.

2015. *2016 Republican Presidential Debate*. Performed by Dr. Ben Carson. QuickenLoans Arena, Cleveland. August 6.

Cell Press. 2008. *Fish Choose Their Leader By Consensus*. November 14. Accessed May 21, 2016. https://www.sciencedaily.com/releases/2008/11/081113140310.htm.

Center for Security Policy. 2015. *Poll of U.S. Muslims Reveals Ominous Levels Of Support For Islamic Supremacists' Doctrine of Shariah, Jihad*. Poll Results, Center for Security Policy, Washington: Center for Security Policy.

Chetty, Raj, Hendren, Nathaniel, Kline, Patrick, and Sues, Emmanual. 2014. *Where is the Land of Opportunity? The Geography of Intergenerational Mobility in the United States*. Study, Harvard, Boston: Raj Chetty.

Cialdini, Robert. 2008. *Influence: Science and Practice*. 5th. Boston: Allyn and Bacon.

Erickson, Erick. 2015. *I Have Disinvited Donald Trump to the Red State Gathering*. August 7. Accessed May 21, 2016. http://www.redstate.com/erick/2015/08/07/i-have-disinvited-donald-trump-to-the-redstate-gathering/.

—. 2015. *This is a Brilliant Move by Donald Trump* . December 7. Accessed May 21, 2016. http://www.redstate.com/erick/2015/12/07/this-is-a-brilliant-move-by-donald-trump/.

Gerber, Alan S., Donald P. Green, and Christopher W. Larimer. 2008. "'Social Pressure and Voter Turnout: Evidence from a Largescale Field Experiment." *American Political Science Review* 102 (1): 33-48.

Gilbert, Dan. 2004. *The Surprising Science of Happiness*. Video. Produced by TED. Performed by Dan Gilbert.

Goldberg, Jonah. 2015. *No Movement That Embraces Trump Can Call Itself Conservative* . September 6. Accessed May 21, 2016. http://www.nationalreview.com/article/423607/donald-trump-conservative-movement-jonah-goldberg.

Healy, Patrick, and Jonathan Martin. 2016. *For Republicans, Mounting Fears of Lasting Split.* January 9. Accessed May 21, 2016. http://www.nytimes.com/2016/01/10/us/politics/for-republicans-mounting-fears-of-lasting-split.html?_r=0.

Hennessy, William T. 2015. "Do You Really Want Your Principles to Win?" *Hennessy's View*. August 10. Accessed May 16, 2016. http://hennessysview.com/2015/08/10/do-you-really-want-your-principles-to-win/.

—. 2010. "Is Glenn Beck Helping?" *Hennessy's View*. September 21. Accessed May 16, 2016. http://hennessysview.com/2010/09/21/is-glenn-beck-helping/.

Hook, Janet. 2016. *Donald Trump Holds 15-Point Lead Ahead of Republican Rivals in Indiana Poll.* May 1. Accessed May 21, 2016. http://www.wsj.com/articles/donald-trump-holds-15-point-lead-ahead-of-republican-rivals-in-indiana-poll-1462107603.

Howe, Neil, and William Strauss. 1997. *The Fourth Turning*. New York: Random House.

Hunt, Ben. 2015. "I Know It Was You, Fredo." *Epsilon Theory*. December 8. Accessed May 21, 2016. http://www.salientpartners.com/epsilon-theory/i-know-it-was-you-fredo/.

Isenstadt, Alex. 2016. *Inside Cruz's camp, confidence crumbles*. April 30. Accessed May 21, 2016. http://www.politico.com/story/2016/04/ted-cruz-campaign-nervous-222675.

King, Steven, and Stanley Kubrick. 1980. *The Shining*. Directed by Stanley Kubrick. Performed by Jack Nicholson, Shelly Duvall and Danny Lloyd.

Krauthammer, Charles, interview by Brett Baier. 2015. "Special Report." *Special Report*. Fox News. August 25.

Leonhardt, David. 2012. "A Different Poll Question: Who Do You Think Will Win?" *New York Times*. November 1. Accessed May 21, 2016. http://www.nytimes.com/2012/11/02/us/politics/a-better-poll-question-to-predict-the-election.html?_r=0.

Limbaugh, David. 2016. "Suggested Cruz Campaign Reboot: Show, Don't Tell." *Townhall*. February 23. Accessed May 16, 2016. http://townhall.com/columnists/davidlimbaugh/2016/02/23/suggested-cruz-campaign-reboot-show-dont-tell-n2123362.

Lizza, Ryan. 2016. "Ted Cruz's Iowa Mailers Are More Fraudulent Than Everyone Thinks." *The New Yorker*. January 31. Accessed May 21, 2016. http://www.newyorker.com/news/news-desk/ted-cruzs-iowa-mailers-are-more-fraudulent-than-everyone-thinks.

Morrissey, Edward. 2016. *Trump's Hard Truth for the GOP: Conservatism Doesn't Matter*. May 5. Accessed may 21, 2016. http://www.thefiscaltimes.com/Columns/2016/05/05/Trump-s-Hard-Truth-GOP-Conservatism-Doesn-t-Matter.

Newmyer, Tory. 2016. "The Long, Dark Twilight of the Political Establishment." *Fortune*. February 19. Accessed May 21, 2016. http://fortune.com/2016/02/19/trump-sanders-cruz-political-establishment/.

Noonan, Peggy. 2016. *Simple Patriotism Trumps Ideology*. April 28. Accessed May 21, 2016. http://www.wsj.com/articles/simple-patriotism-trumps-ideology-1461886199.

—. 2016. *Trump and the Rise of the Unprotected*. February 25. Accessed May 21, 2016. http://www.wsj.com/articles/trump-and-the-rise-of-the-unprotected-1456448550.

Politico. 2016. "South Carolina Presidential Primary Results." *Politico*. February. Accessed May 21, 2016. http://www.politico.com/2016-election/results/map/president/south-carolina.

Rasmussen Reports. 2016. *Trump Change*. May 6. Accessed

May 21, 2016. http://www.rasmussenreports.com/public_content/politics/elections/election_2016/trump_change.

Rothschild, David and Wolfers, Justin. 2012. *Forecasting Elections: Voter Intentions versus Expectations**. Study, New York: ResearchDRM.

Schleifer, Theodore, and Eric Bradner. 2016. *Ted Cruz's Indiana plan: Throw everything at the wall and see what sticks* . April 29. Accessed May 21, 2016. http://www.cnn.com/2016/04/28/politics/ted-cruz-carly-fiorina-indiana-plan/index.html.

Sinek, Simon. 2014. *How Great Leaders Make You Feel Safe*. Performed by Simon Sinek. March.

—. 2014. *Leaders Eat Last*. New York: Penguin.

Spades, Ace of. 2105. *Jeb Bush Threatens to Kill the Republican Party*. December 16. Accessed May 21, 2016. http://ace.mu.nu/archives/360610.php.

Teisch, Steve. 1979. *Breaking Away*. Directed by Peter Yates. Performed by Dennis Quaid, Daniel Stern Dennis Christopher.

Trende, Sean. 2016. *Cruz, Trump, and the Missing White Voter*. January 28. Accessed May 21, 2016. http://www.realclearpolitics.com/articles/2016/01/28/cruz_trump_and_the_missing_white_voters_129465.html.

—. 2013. *The Case of the Missing White Voter - Revisited*. June 21. Accessed May 21, 2016. http://www.realclearpolitics.com/articles/2013/06/

21/the_case_of_the_missing_white_voters_revisited_118893.html.

2016. *2016 Republican Presidential Debate*. Performed by Donald J. Trump. Reagan Library, Simi Valley. September 16.

Trump, Donald J. and McIver, Meredith. 2004. *How To Get Rich*. New York: RandomHouse.

Trump, Donald J. 2015. *Crippled America: How to Make America Great Again*. New York: Threshold Editions.

Wagner, Ann, interview by William T. Hennessy. 2012. *Interview with Ann Wagner* (August).

Will, George F. 2009. *America's Bad Jeans*. April 16. Accessed May 21, 2016. http://www.washingtonpost.com/wp-dyn/content/article/2009/04/15/AR2009041502861.html.

Williamson, Kevin. 2016. *Our Post-Literate Politics*. January 26. Accessed May 21, 2016. http://www.nationalreview.com/article/430227/donald-trump-supporters-establishment-books.

World Net Daily. 2015. *Phyllis Schlafly: Trump Is "Last Hope for America"*. December 20. Accessed May 21, 2016. http://www.wnd.com/2015/12/top-conservative-trump-is-last-hope-for-america/.

ABOUT THE AUTHOR

William Hennessy is a Navy submarine veteran and author.

He blogs at www.hennessysview.com and
www.billhennessy.com.
He has five children and step-children, including two U.S. Navy sailors, a teacher, and a firefighter.
Bill lives in Eureka, Missouri, with his wife Angela.

This is Bill's fifth book. Other books by
William T. Hennessy:

The Conservative Manifesto (Right Press, 1993)
Zen Conservatism (Right Press, 2009)
Weaving the Roots (HarperCollins, 2010)
Fight to Evolve (Coalition for Safer Drinking, 2016)

Made in the USA
San Bernardino, CA
04 July 2016